texas country style

"Calhoun and Snortum have wrapped their arms around all that makes Texas country more than a place—it's a style of living and decorating suited to an urban escape artist as well as a cattle king."
—Lynette Jennings
Lynette Jennings Design and *HouseSmart*

D. ALAN CALHOUN

PHOTOGRAPHY BY
MARTY SNORTUM

texas country style

GIBBS·SMITH
P
PUBLISHER
SALT LAKE CITY

First Edition
04 03 02 01   4 3 2 1

Published by
Gibbs Smith, Publisher
PO Box 667
Layton, UT 84041
Orders: 800-748-5439
www.gibbs-smith.com

Design by Chen Design Associates

Printed in Hong Kong

Library of Congress Cataloging-in-Publication Data

Calhoun, D. Alan.
Texas country style / text by D. Alan Calhoun ;
photography by Marty Snortum. — 1st ed.
p. cm.

ISBN 1-58685-013-X

1. Interior decoration — United States — History — 20th century.
2. Decoration and ornament, Rustic — Texas — Influence.
   I. Snortum, Marty. II. Title.

NK2004.C35 2001
747.2164—dc21   2001000863

For Jett, a fellow Texan.

— D. A. C.

To Raymond and Herta E. Snortum.
There are other parents, but I wouldn't
have chosen any other. Thanks for all.

— M. S.

CONTENTS

PREFACE

When I was three years old, my father bought his first new car—a two-tone Chevrolet with air-conditioning. I can vividly remember my family's shopping trip for that Chevy. It was a sunny morning and rows of shiny new Chevrolets reflected the checkered flags strung above them. A salesman in a suit and hat gave my sister and me wooden yo-yos with the Chevrolet crest emblazoned on the side. My parents studied the window stickers on the cars, quickly moving away from the Impalas and finding our price range to be more among the Bel-Airs. And on that day we found our Bel-Air sitting in the corner of the lot under a large metal awning. This was the one. The whole family knew it, and my dad hurriedly ushered the salesman away from our excitement to make his deal. By that afternoon, our old coupe was sitting on the OK used-car lot and our new Chevy was parked under the carport of our little ranch-style house. Within days we headed out on our first adventure in that car: we were off to see the Alamo.

As we left our little east Texas town for San Antonio, Dad made one stop—at the local Perry Brothers five-and-dime store. There he bought two little pillows that, in those pre-child-restraint-law days, were just the right height to let me sit next to him and look down that baby blue hood at my first stretches of Texas two-lane. We drove along with our windows proudly rolled up in the middle of August, letting the whole world know that we were air-conditioned.

As the miles rolled by, my dad tried to hold my interest by talking of Davy Crockett and the other heroes of the Alamo. I'm sure that his historical overview of the battle more closely followed the John Wayne version that the family had seen at the Pine Top Drive-In Theater than what the history book might have said. But I have to admit that I was excited at the possibility that I might encounter my own television-induced version of Davy at our destination. To my disappointment, there was no Fess Parker waiting for me at the Alamo. But there was something different, something that has stuck with me for a lifetime.

I clearly remember watching my father remove his Stetson before opening the big front door of the Alamo for me to pass through. He stopped me at the threshold to remove the baseball cap from my head, and then lifted me up to carry me inside. A hushed crowd milled around cases filled with mementos, and Rangers guarded the Lone Star flag. I kept asking if they had Davy Crockett's coonskin cap in one of those cases, but no, it wasn't there.

At age three, I didn't understand any of the history that happened there, but I somehow knew that I was in a special place. It was there that my father explained to me that I, too, was a Texan. Most Texans can tell you when and where they became aware of this second nationality. And then it becomes something you carry with you like a lucky charm, making you feel special, as if it were some sort of divine inheritance. Being from Texas becomes part of your identity.

To this day, I cannot pass through San Antonio without stopping to pay my respects there at the Alamo. Since that first visit when my father carried me through the door, I have lived with a passion for my state, trying to explore all of the things that define her. Like a gypsy in cowboy boots, I have roamed her roads and flown her skies. I once had a girlfriend who would plant her bare feet against the dashboard of my old van as she colored in all of the highways we had traveled on an old road map. She colored away with that yellow marker until our map was so tattered that it began to look like a pirate's map, and maybe it was just that—a treasure map. Our treasure was not hard to find: peaches that we picked near Fredericksburg, cold Lone Star beer that we drank in the biergartens of New Braunfels, and barbecue that we purchased from a roadside stand all proved to be our silver. The clear streams of central Texas, the awesome beauty of west Texas, and pony rides along the sandy beaches of the Texas coast were our gold.

Photo courtesy of the Calhoun family.

Photo courtesy of D. Alan Calhoun

I have tried to throw myself into discovering Texas's treasure of people as well, individuals springing from a variety of cultures and comprising a cast of characters that have created a number of adventures along the road. You need no map to find them.

My wanderlust for the state has never diminished. This long odyssey within its borders eventually led me into the business of collecting, designing, and selling what might be called the "look of Texas" in my furniture manufacturing business and as creative director for Antèks, a home-furnishings and accessories retailer. But this Texas style was not created by me. It was handed down for me to work with from the many people who came to Texas before me and unwittingly created a Texas style that would last for more than a 150 years.

It has been forty summers since that August road trip in my father's new car. And in this, my forty-third summer, I drove my three-year-old son to the Alamo in my Chevrolet. I removed his little baseball cap and lifted him onto my arm as we passed through that same old pair of doors my father carried me through. We moved around slowly, as I tried to give a tour that a three-year-old would appreciate. He really didn't have that much to say, and I began to fear boredom. As I took him by the hand and moved toward the exit door, I said, "This is the way out, son." Then I felt a slight resistance against my hand as I heard Jett say, "No, Dad, I don't want to go yet. I like it here."

I let go of his little hand and followed him back into the main part of the building, and with his baseball cap in my hand, watched as he strolled around, looking the place over for a second time. Perhaps it was just that the air-conditioning felt good to him. But I would like to think that maybe I was watching one more little Texan soul awaken in August.

GONE TO TEXAS

As we roll along the highway heading southeast, west Texas opens itself up to us like a giant road map that just keeps unfolding endlessly. We top a rise in the road and are met with yet one more horizon in the distance to remind us just how big this land is. Photographer Marty Snortum rides alongside me in the cab of the pickup truck, and talk remains small as we each soak up the country on our own terms. Marty and I are on a mission. We have set out to experience and photograph homes that capture one part of the Texas lifestyle — the art of country living, Texas style — country living in a state big enough to be its own country.

Texas is a land of many landscapes. Starting out from El Paso, we travel through rocky terrain dotted with mesquite and cactus. Occasional towns are divided by many miles. Off to our right, distant mountains give us some idea of where Mexico lies. From one viewpoint, this is a region where one can find perspective. The broad horizons make life's daily issues and petty problems seem small and pointless; man's insignificance in the "big" picture becomes somehow comforting. From another view, this wide expanse is just too intimidating and makes us feel naked in the vast openness of land. On this day we are enjoying the broad horizons.

I am a native Texan while Marty is a transplanted one. You don't have to be born here to call yourself a Texan, but you do have to pay some dues. Being out here on the road, coming to terms with the size of this place, is one of those payments. Right now, Marty seems a little overwhelmed.

2

Approaching Ozona, the needle on the gas gauge finally gets my attention and we wheel off the road. As the truck gulps down high-octane, I look up and down the main drag of this little town. Ozona is not much different from many other small Texas towns these days. There are a couple of gas stations and places to eat. There's where the car dealership used to be; over here I see what must have been a hardware store once upon a time. In many of these small towns, the commerce of mom and pop has gone the way of the buffalo. With dusk beginning to fall, I notice the neon pop to life on one of the little motels that line what used to be the main highway through town. Wait until deer hunting season, though; every "NO Vacancy" sign in town will be lit and this sleepy town will be wide awake and dressed in camouflage, with hundreds of unlucky mule deer strapped across the hoods of SUVs.

Ozona is the county seat of Crockett County, and appropriately so, has a statue of Davy Crockett guarding the courthouse square. As we pull off of the square, I see Davy standing there, slightly larger than life, and, like most Texans, I start to swell with pride. Then, completely unsolicited, I go into about a forty-mile-long oration about Crockett and his band of volunteers who came from Tennessee to Texas to join in the movement for independence from Mexico. Eventually all died in the Battle at the Alamo. In one of his final letters written home to Tennessee, Davy described Texas to a friend. He simply stated, "I am traveling through God's country."

I finally turn to Marty to see his response to my display of Texas knowledge and all he has to say is, "Fritos?" as he extends the bag to me. "How much farther to where we're spending the night?" he questions. I reluctantly tell him that we are still about four hours from our night's stop. "Man, this God's country of yours is just too big!" he replies.

While I'm not ready to say Texas is "too big," I will concede that it is a really big place. Texas covers 266,807 square miles, to be exact. El Paso County, where Marty and I are from, is larger than the state of Rhode Island. Adjacent Hudspeth County is larger than the state of Connecticut. It is farther from my home in El Paso to Texarkana, Texas, all the way across the state, than it is from Paris to Warsaw!

TAKING THE INSIDE OUT

The landscape vistas and homestead settings have everything to do with the country way of life. Texas retains enough of the southern slowness and graciousness that country folk actually take the time to pause and enjoy the view. Whether on a covered porch, in chairs under a shade tree, or on a picnic blanket down by the river, Texans enjoy feeling surrounded by nature. These favorite outdoor spots become extensions of the house, either literally or figuratively.

For instance, one family has automatic deer feeders just behind their house, set to throw out corn each evening at 5:30. By 6:00, the family gathers for refreshments on the back deck to watch the show of deer that have fallen into the same schedule as the family. Taking the family outside this way makes a rich setting for their sharing of the day's tales and for acknowledging the beauty by which they are lucky enough to be surrounded.

It's hard to walk past this comfortable-looking rocker as it teases us in the afternoon shade.

The Guadalupe River of the Texas Hill Country.

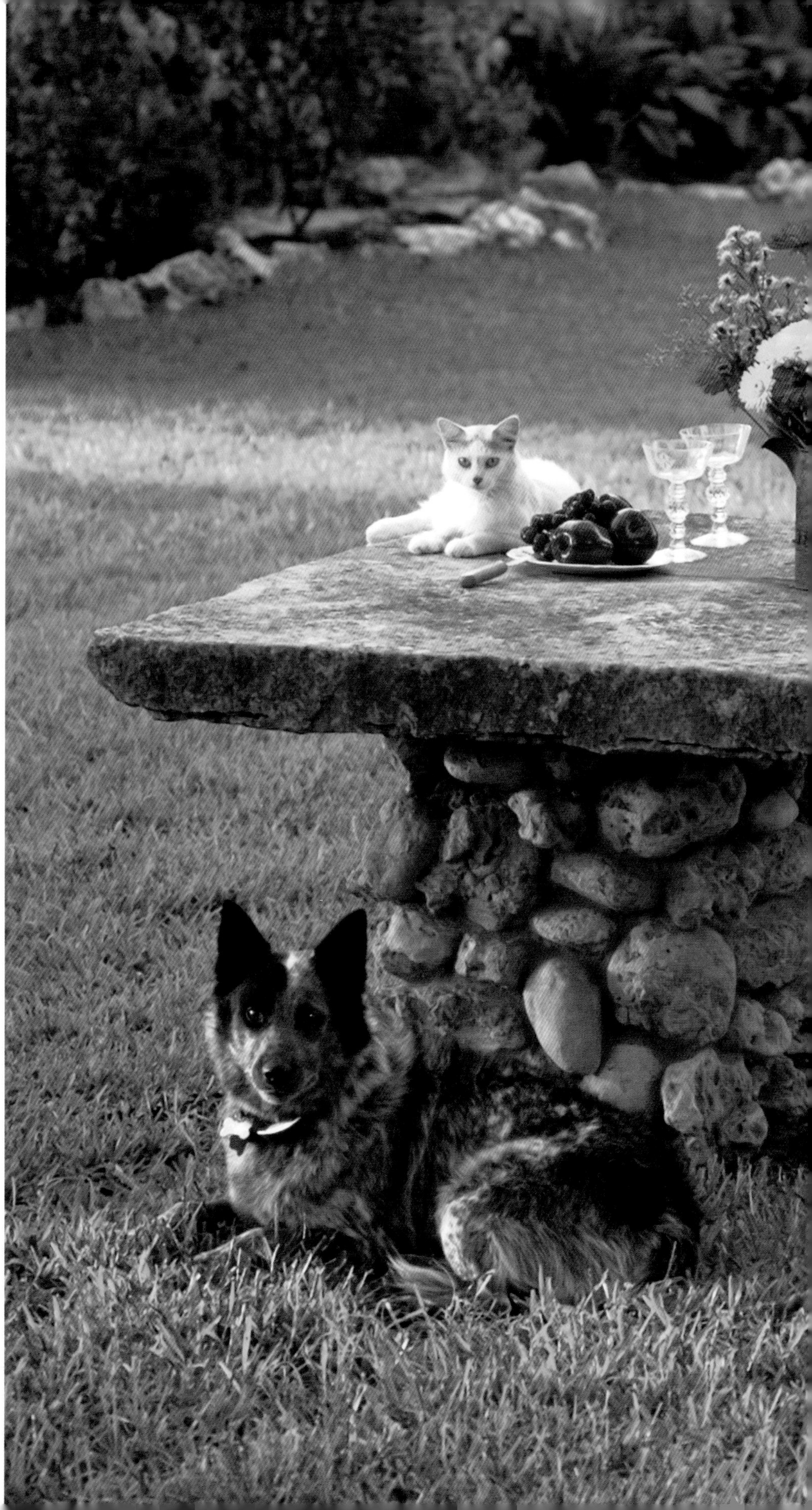

Jake and Pearl enjoy a Hill Country afternoon.

What does all this have to do with Texas style, you wonder? It's that even as huge and diverse as Texas is, with as many cultures and landscapes as exist here, there are elements born out of its history and settlement and economic development that form the foundation of the way Texans live today and even how they decorate their homes. And, in fact, Texas's great size and openness have a tremendous influence on country style as well, for it is the isolation, independence and distance from one house to the next that keep this region relatively free of oppressive building codes, allowing an enhanced freedom of expression.

Summer wildflowers aglow on the YO Ranch, near Mountain Home.

WIDELY VARIED LANDSCAPES

Once the idea of Texas's overwhelming expanse is digested, acknowledging its different geographic regions is probably the greatest factor in grasping the Texas lifestyle. Hollywood's depictions of Texas have, for the most part, shown the desolation of west Texas, this country Marty and I are cruising across right now. But Texas is much more than the sagebrush and cactus of John Ford's movies.

The piney woods of northeast Texas slowly evolve into the almost jungle-like conditions of the Big Thicket region as one moves south along the eastern boundary. Farther south are swampland and bayous, then the warm beaches of the Gulf Coast. West of those same piney woods is rich, dark-soiled farmland, then the prairie spreads open just west of Fort Worth. Many say that this is where the West begins, where prairie turns to rocky, mesquite-covered ranching country before the land drops into the Permian Basin region, the floor of an ancient sea now covered with hundreds of thousands of oil wells, pumping away as if their rocking motion were some sort of life-support system keeping the state alive. West of that, the land climbs into west Texas above the caprock elevation that divides the high desert and the high prairie country. Here the southernmost tip of the Rocky Mountains combines with high desert to show just how harsh land can be. The Guadalupe Mountains and the amazing Big Bend country offer some of the nation's most inspiring vistas, as the Rio Grande cuts her slow path to the ocean, showing all where Texas ends and Mexico begins. Folks out here love to say that this is not the end of the world, but you can see the end of the world from here.

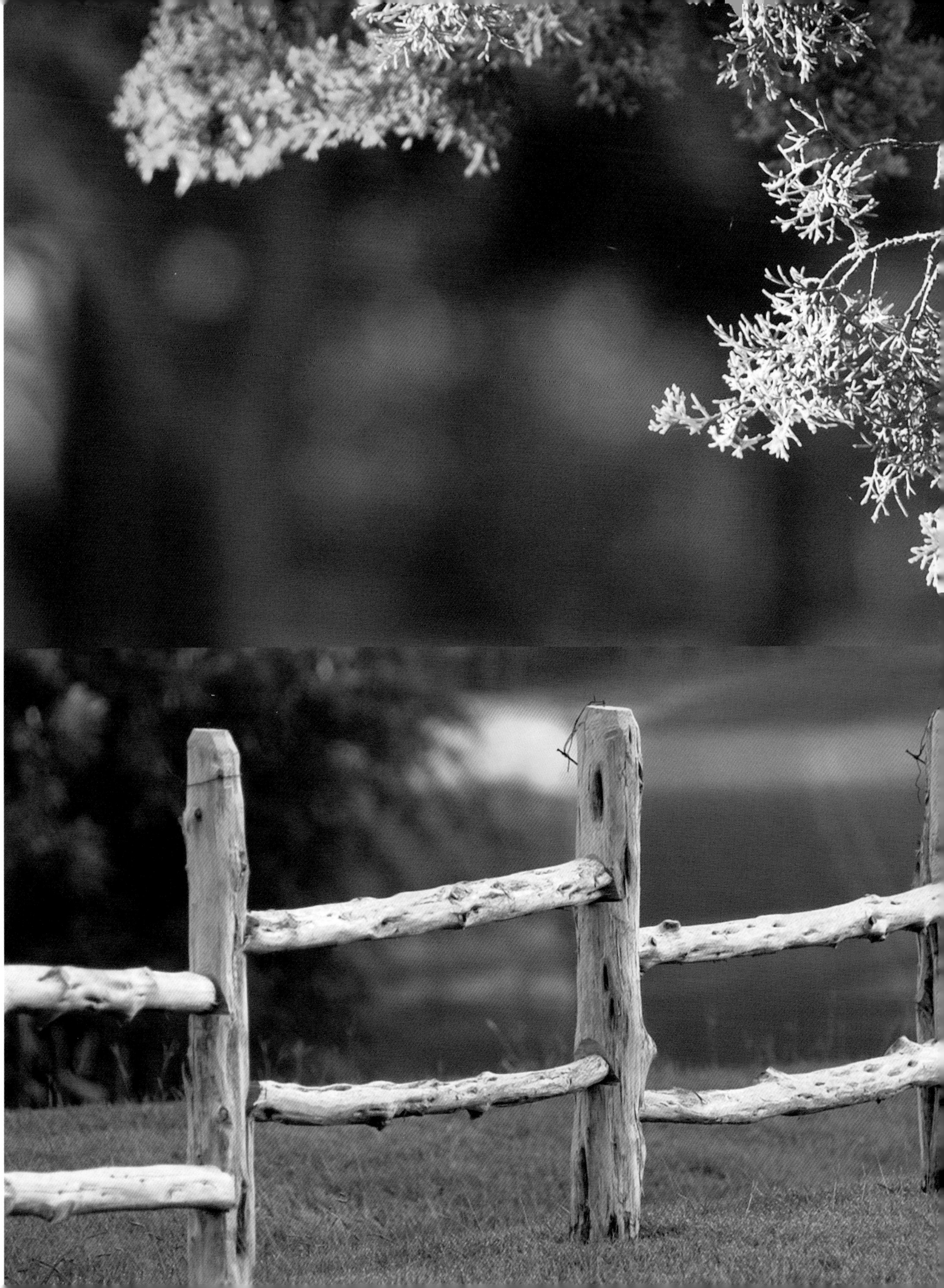

The scent of the Texas Hills.

The Panhandle is the northernmost region of Texas, an area comprised of grasslands, wheat fields, and even more desert country. Route 66 cuts through this area, where conquistadors once searched for Eldorado. But the gold here today is the small towns —divided by endless straight stretches of two-lane—with their skating rinks and dance halls where legends like Buddy Holly and Bob Wills faced their first audiences.

Central Texas is known as the Hill Country. Here, rolling hills covered with oak give shade to yucca, cactus, and an unbelievable explosion of wildflowers. Clear, flowing rivers and streams travel among clean, well-organized towns founded by pioneer immigrants. The southernmost tip of Texas is known as "the Valley." Its climate, with the intensity of Mexico just to the west and the usually calm Gulf of Mexico to the east, allows for lush fruit groves and tropical palms to dominate the flora.

14

Texas bounty for both the eyes and the dinner table.

Found in each region are sophisticated, high-energy cities—Dallas, Houston, Austin, and San Antonio, to name a few. Texas can be as hip and cosmopolitan as any other state. But it just seems that country living has to prevail in country this big. And not just country living by necessity. A large percentage of people trapped in suburbia by professional commitments maintain a rural retreat of some kind. Many high-ranking professionals who were once small-town kids escaped their country roots to fulfill dreams in the city, but now they find themselves needing to reconnect with something that they may not completely understand but cannot resist. Because they are able to afford dual lifestyles, those tailored suits give way to jeans and scuffed-up cowboy boots come Friday, when a $150 trip to the salon is covered by a beat-up cowboy hat and the Range Rover gets parked behind the barn in favor of a rusty old truck as the weekend's transportation.

The art of escape takes many shapes and styles, from very elegant living in the most remote of settings, to saying good-bye to city life and truly embracing the rustic lifestyle. Two themes that characterize Texas country living are artful living and personal freedom. The latter is a principle upon which Texas was built. The founding fathers built Texas out of the quest for true freedom, the kind one is willing to die for. These principles do not fade; they are passed from generation to generation. One way we act out these principles is by valuing the freedom to live the way we want without necessarily needing the approval, or sometimes even the companionship, of others.

The classic windmill is a common sight on the Texas prairie.

In the early days of westward migration, the frontier was a constantly changing line. Areas of new settlement would fill up quickly. As the stories of the land and opportunities of Texas began to spread, it became common to find homestead cabins in Tennessee, Kentucky, and along the Ohio River abandoned, with the slogan "Gone to Texas" painted on the front door. On this evening, after crossing such a distance of west Texas desert and reaching the paradise of the Texas Hills, Marty and I are happy to find ourselves "gone to Texas" too.

By this time it is dark and Marty and I, nearing our destination, have finally managed to escape the interstate to a proper two-lane road. We are winding along, following the Guadalupe River in the heart of Hill Country. We are in no hurry now as we decompress, letting go of the long day's road race. I roll the windows down and hear water falling down river steps, cuffing its way through the Texas Hills. An occasional break in the cypress trees and the glasslike surface of the Guadalupe give the summer moon a perfect mirror in which to admire itself. Davy was right: we are in "God's country," and I guess only a Texan would have the gall to declare even God as one of our own residents.

TEXAS STYLE EVOLVES

UNDER SIX FLAGS

the influences

Country living in Texas can take many shapes and fashions. From lake house to ranch house, Texans love their getaways. With many different geographic regions in the state, natural materials available for construction and for fashioning furniture vary as much as the landscape features.

In Texas, country living is probably more about expressing personal freedom than it is about expressing personal style. And that, after all, is what this great state was founded on: the freedom to live as one wished. Much blood was shed to make Texas free, and today Texans still honor the sacrifices made by their founding fathers. Some of that homage is paid by the way Texans live and is evidenced as Texas pride.

Many influences have affected what Texas style is all about. From the indigenous peoples to those who immigrated to the state, the area has been sculpted not only by nature but also by many hands. The region of Texas has existed under six different flags—Spain, France, Mexico, Republic of Texas (the Lone Star), the Confederacy, and the United States—the influences of which can be found in all forms of country living within the state.

In addition, strong stylistic influences evolved around the ranching and cattle industry, as well as the oil industry. The unusual thing about Texas country style today is that it exhibits measures of all these influences. So, not only is country style affected by the landscape and naturally available materials, but also by the historical development of the region and the groups of people who were responsible for Texas's settlement and economic growth. In most regions of the United States where historical groups imbue architectural or design styles, contemporary home style reflects just one or two of these influences. In Texas country style, people give nod to all of the influences, creating a tastefully eclectic blend that opens wide the door to expressing personal freedom.

Wild turkey beards collected from a lifetime of hunting holiday birds, which were strung up by the hunter on the day before his death, adorn the fireplace of Pony Creek Ranch. Owner Jim Berry displays these trophies of his father's passion for hunting not in sadness but in tribute to a man who loved and lived in the Texas outdoors.

The Virgin de Guadalupe, patron saint of Mexico, seems to stand guard over those who choose to relax in this traditional Mexican jardín *(flower garden).*

EUROPEAN STYLE UNDER THE SPANISH FLAG

The first people to lay claim to this land were the Spanish. While there were Native inhabitants before the Spaniards arrived, their philosophy was that people did not own the land; they simply lived on it. Spanish efforts to colonize revolved around the Catholic Church's system of missions. As Spanish padres organized Native people to construct missions, the region's first serious architecture evolved. These padres worked with ideas of design from their homeland, taking advantage of native stone, adobe, and timber. The Spanish influence on Texas style was firmly planted.

(Inset) *The home of H. Park and Martina Kerr in El Paso exhibits the best of traditional Mexican colonial décor. The side table, with its architectural details, hints at Martina's occupation: a top El Paso architect.*

24

Though the use of adobe has generally given way to conventional construction these days, Spanish influences can still be found in many contemporary buildings. Carved stonework reminiscent of the Mediterranean area and the use of tiles (both glazed and unglazed), heavy pine woodwork, and forged-iron hardware are all examples of how Spanish influence lives on in Texas architecture today.

In the world of interior furnishings, the legacy of Spain also thrived. The furniture used by the Spanish padres and settlers was rarely brought from home. It was constructed in the fashion of the Spanish homeland using materials at hand, mainly abundant Texas pine. Spanish furniture is more European in silhouette—at times quite ornate, but always maintaining focus on function. The Spanish carpenters paid attention to detail in things such as carving and the elements of construction and joinery. The Spanish created a heavy, rugged look in furniture that certainly relates to European influence and makes a bolder statement. Iron, though a precious commodity at the time of the frontier, found its way into the early furniture in the form of beautifully forged hinges, pulls, and clavos (nail heads). Iron was also forged into lamp bases, chandeliers, and candelabras. While a necessary material for lighting fixtures, much of the ironwork was ornate and worked in the tradition of the old-world blacksmiths, many times looking almost medieval in style

The look of Spanish living in Texas was distinctively European, especially in home environments that were elegantly furnished with things brought by ship from the homeland, such as tapestries, art, and silver utilitarian objects. All set against the rustic backdrop of frontier Texas, it was a warm yet worldly look that can easily be called upon for inspiration today, especially at the present time, when much new construction is reflecting a Mediterranean influence.

This hand-forged iron chair seems to be returning to the earth as it rusts away in a forgotten corner of the garden. Perhaps it is someone's secret spot to hide for a moment and reflect on the beauty of growing things.

A LITTLE FRENCH PERSUASION

A flag whose shadow at times overlapped the Spanish bandera was that of France. The French entrée into Texas came more as a result of expansion from nearby Louisiana for trade purposes with the Natives than from what might be called true colonization. Even so, this encroachment eventually led to war between Spain and France to finally establish a boundary between the two.

The French forts and trading posts introduced the log structure into East Texas. Log homes were pretty much the only option in this thickly wooded part of the state. A log cabin might be built in haste to simply provide one room of shelter. Later, a second cabin of equal size would be built, perhaps ten feet from the first but in line with the original. These two cabins would then be connected by a covered porch, forming what became a Texas classic, the dogtrot cabin (referring to the fact that a dog could trot right through the middle of the structure). Log homes are still abundant in Texas, with log being a popular choice for second homes and retreats.

MEXICO'S EVERLASTING SPELL

In August of 1821, Mexico declared its independence from Spain, and with Texas having been declared a part of the Republic of Mexico in 1813, yet another flag was raised over Texas soil. While Mexico's control over Texas was relatively short-lived, it was during this period that Texas began to really form her identity.

It is obvious today that the Mexican influence on style and design has a direct link to the previously discussed Spanish influences. However, the Mexican home and its furnishings were more utilitarian than those of the Spanish. In many cases architectural embellishments were created with paint or carved woodwork rather than the stonework of the Spanish masons. Simple details were added to homes at nominal cost, in many cases by the owners themselves.

The traditional style of Mexico remains a major part of Texas country living. Left is a colorful folk art accent. On this page is the dining room of Hacienda Calhoun, near El Paso. A stagecoach stop built in 1859, today it is a perfect example of the lasting influence of Mexican taste and tradition. Sitting on the original Camino Real, the home has hosted such notables as William Bonny (alias Billy the Kid). Fine Mexican religious art and hand-forged iron mix cordially with elements of the West and the ever-present Texas lone star.

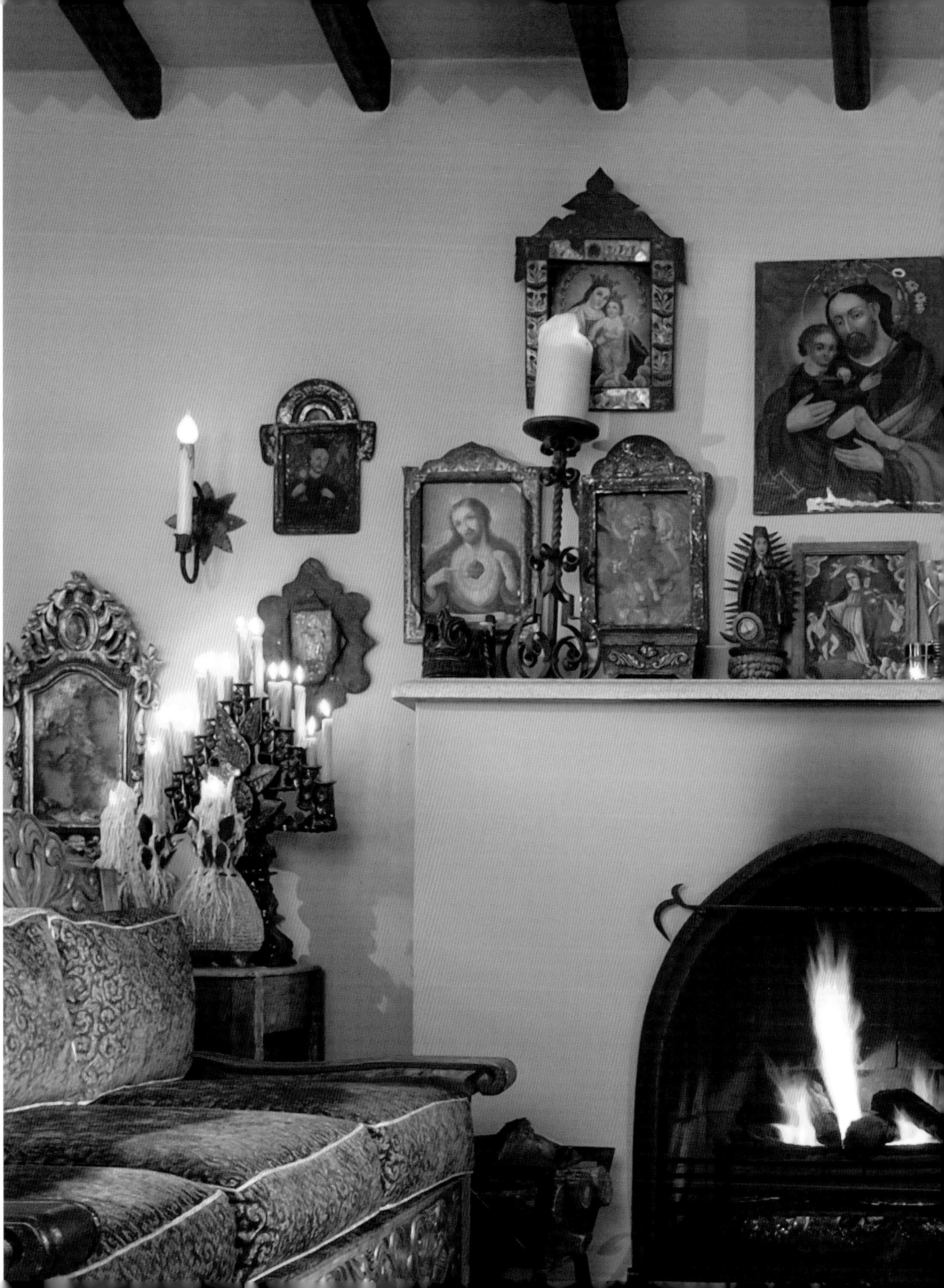

The religious icons of Mexico not only symbolize sacred beliefs but also represent a folk art that can vary from primitive to high art. These combine with rich fabrics, heavy woods and forged iron to create a setting that, while reminiscent of Europe, is a classical reminder of Mexico's occupation of Texas.

A wheel that once graced a Mexican ox cart finds a new life when converted into a chandelier for the YO Ranch near Mountain Home.

Brightly colored bowls have a rustic Mexican flavor that can add color to any kitchen or table.

The adobe construction of Hacienda Calhoun is typical for most of west Texas. The mud home can be dressed up by the use of simple wooden and painted adornments.

Native stone and sticks likely gathered around the building site work in perfect and simple unity for this portal.

Certainly the greatest common denominator in Mexican architecture is the use of adobe, or mud brick, sometimes finished off in a smooth coating of stucco. Obviously, in a land of few trees, one has to turn to the earth itself for building material, and in a region known for extreme temperatures, adobe became the most commonly used home construction material in south-central and west Texas. From the plainest homestead to urban development in areas such as San Antonio de Bexar, adobe prevailed, and the flat, low Mexican hacienda style of architecture became the norm. (Interestingly, during the Victorian period, it was common to see whitewashed adobe homes trimmed with the moldings and woodwork common to urban settings of the 1890s, thus creating an interesting mix of traditional and new.)

In today's energy-conscious world, adobe has met with a renewed interest and popularity. The Mexican influence on furnishings, as well, is more utilitarian but still reflects its Spanish ancestry. Mexican furniture is built on an aesthetic of function and then decorated with paint or by ornate ironwork. It is common to find wood furniture from this settlement period elaborately decorated with hand-painted flowers and designs, with pine and Mexican sabino wood being the most commonly used materials. Mexican furniture has enjoyed a resurgent popularity in recent years, both as collectible and as reproduction furniture pieces.

These "shard art" flowerpots are a fringe form of tramp art.

This guest space in the loft of the barn at Lewis Dickson's LD3 Ranch provides a gallery-like setting for the owner's collections of historic and contemporary Hispanic arts and crafts.

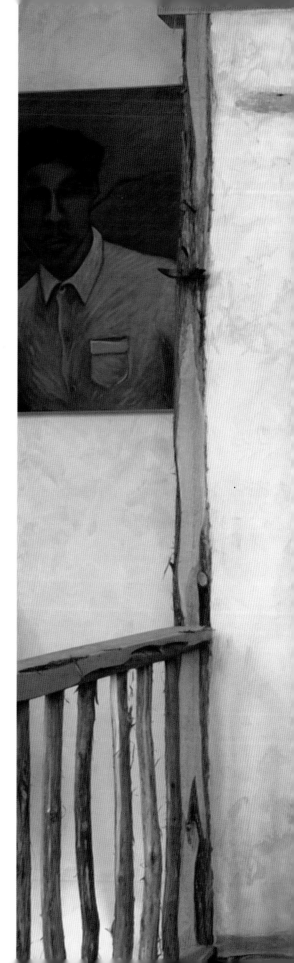

Bright colors prevail in Mexican style, both in painted furniture and in textiles. From the serapes of Saltillo to the rugs of Oaxaca, today Mexican textiles are as fun to collect as to use. This love of bright color must have been inherited from the Aztec and Mayan civilizations that first occupied this country and also expressed themselves with vivid color, probably inspired by the tropical birds of the Yucatán region of Mexico.

Although Texas won independence from Mexico in 1836 after a bitter and legendary war for freedom, Mexican heritage is inherent in many aspects of the Texas lifestyle.

FREE EXPRESSION COMES UNDER THE REPUBLIC

Once Texas became a republic, it began to develop the Texas style that we know today—that is, the visual expression of Texas pride. In Texas schools, it is mandated that all students receive an approved course in Texas history. It is generally in these classrooms that the names of the heroes of this era are first heard by little Texan ears. Names like Travis, Bowie, Crockett, and Houston are tattooed onto our souls, and we begin to understand that to be from Texas is more than just to be from a particular state: it is part of our bloodline.

Under the freedom of the Lone Star flag, Texas flourished. People began to immigrate, bringing a Mulligan's stew of influences on Texas style. The most prevalent immigrant group was the Germans. The earliest German settlement began in 1838 in Austin County. The German immigrants, who employed construction methods typical of Europe (they were exceptionally adept in timber building and stonework) adapted their skills and processes to Texas. They cut Texas limestone and combined it with precise and often ornate woodwork to create beautiful, clean homesteads. The Germans brought with them the traditional post-and-beam construction used for hundreds of years in Europe, as well as log-home construction techniques much more refined than those evidenced in cabins built hastily by earlier pioneers. Many German log homes were so well constructed that, when finances and materials later became available, wood siding was added over the log exterior for a more conventional look. The well-organized towns of Texas's Hill Country are trademarks of German immigration. Towns like Fredericksburg and New Braunfels are still very German, with traditional biergartens and smokehouses, and the German language commonly spoken.

The architecture of the Mike Mullins 4M Ranch combines traditional building materials with a contemporary form—clean lines and beams used decoratively rather than structurally—that whispers of classic Texas ranch headquarters of the nineteenth century.

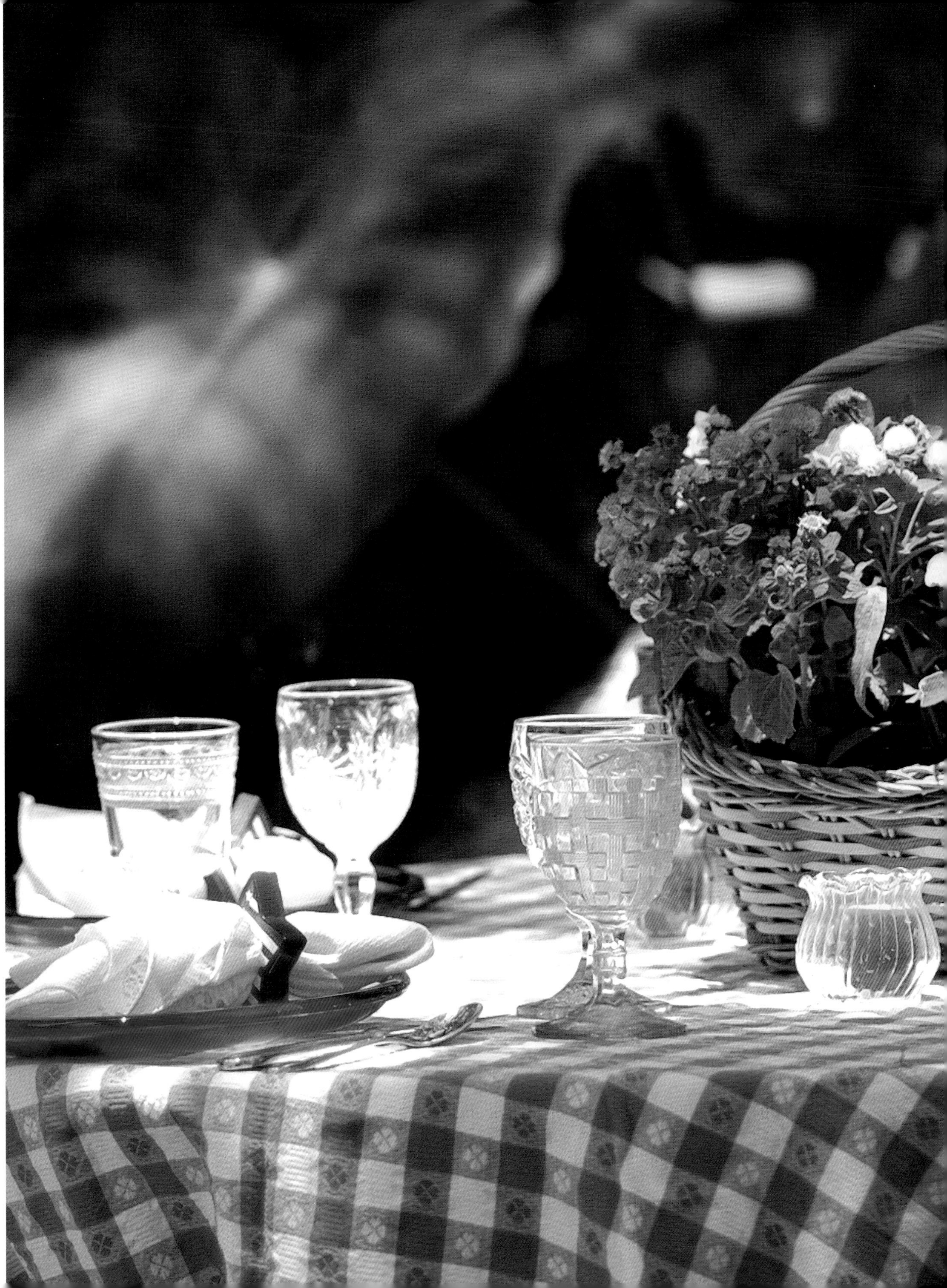

*The graciousness of the southern planta-
tion lifestyle remains influential in Texans'
entertaining as well as in their sense of
luxury at slowing down the pace to enjoy
the refreshing spirit of the outdoors.*

CLASSIC SOUTHERN INFLUENCES
UNDER THE CONFEDERATE FLAG

The eastern part of Texas, having rich soil and being in proximity to the Southern
States, became a natural for cotton crops. When Texas seceded from the Union to
join the South in 1860, yet one more flag waved over Texas—the stars and bars of
the Confederacy. The gentle ways of the South found their way into east Texas and a
few examples of the classic antebellum plantation home even exist there, along with
the log structures of the pioneer lifestyle.

By 1865 the War Between the States had ended and Texas experienced a new type of
migration. Many Southerners, finding they had nothing to return home to after the
war, crossed the Red River and opted for a new life in Texas. At this point, Texas was
about to enter an era that would forever define her in most eyes. Forget King Cotton,
the lowly longhorn was about to take the throne.

This Stetson, with its Carlsbad roll around the brim, commemorates the Texas centennial of 1936. From the author's collection.

The ubiquitous cowboy and bucking bronco icons that has symbolized the Texas lifestyle since the time of the cattle barons comes in a broad range of materials, shapes, and states of refinement.

RANCHO STYLE MAKES
A LONG-TERM STATEMENT

Ranching is the heritage upon which Texas truly built its legend. The well-known Texas longhorn is a descendent of the first Spanish herds of cattle. Those who controlled the Spanish land grants cultivated these cattle more for sustenance than wealth. Within these huge expanses of land, it became impossible to properly manage livestock, so wild herds of cattle developed, as well as wild packs of horses that later became known as mustangs.

There was a period in Texas when it was possible to simply go out and gather these wild cattle and begin the process of ranching. Modeled after the ranchos of Mexico, these earliest ranches were purely utilitarian affairs. Living in a structure of adobe, stone, and log was not much different than living in a barn, because tack, tools, gear, supplies, and sometimes horses were also contained in the shelter. Gathering all of one's belongings into one location was the best protection against marauding bandits of all persuasions.

These earliest headquarters could be built out as needed, one room at a time, in true hacienda fashion. People working in these operations had little need for decoration, as there were many other more important issues at hand, such as staying alive.

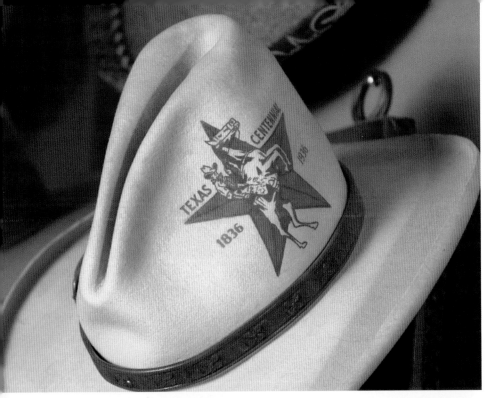

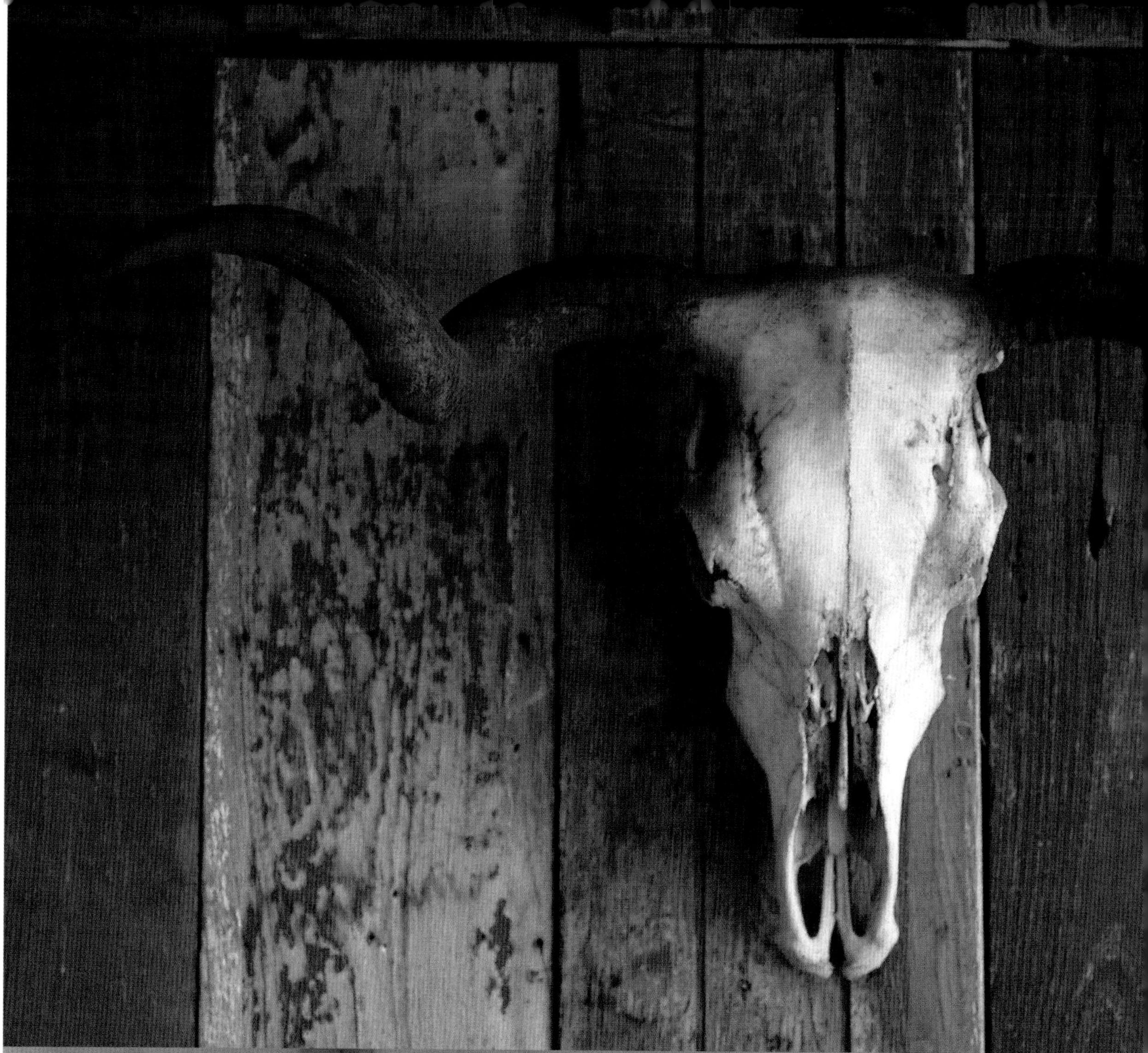

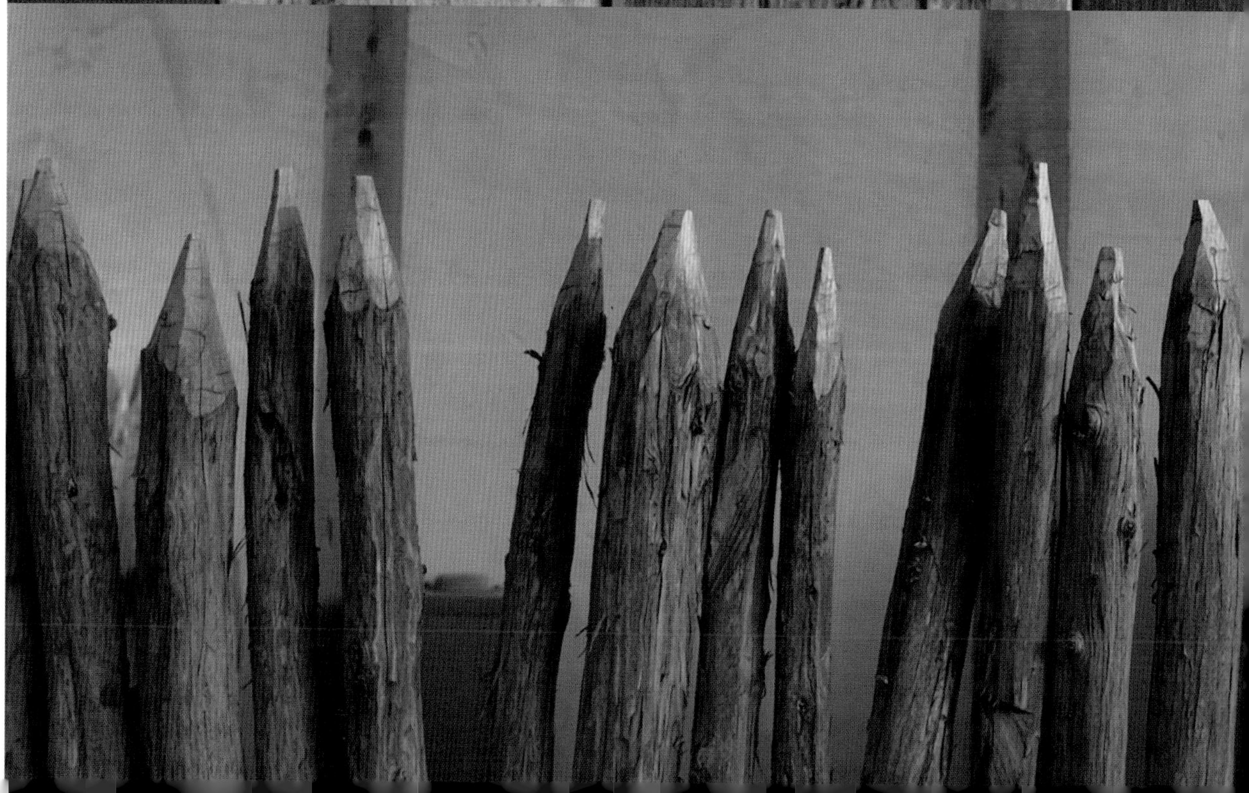

The skull of a Texas longhorn is an artful study in form for those who look beyond its ghostly symbolism.

After the Civil War, growth in the North intensified the need for beef, turning the rangy old steer on the Texas plains into four-legged gold. And with the nearest railheads far north of Texas, the most romantic period of the ranching tradition began— the years of the great drives, where cattle were herded to Kansas and then shipped by rail to points north and east. The cattle-drive era really only lasted a few years, but these few years created the identity of the American cowboy. Legendary names like Goodnight and Chisholm were etched into the stone of western history and lore. But once rail lines connected the Lone Star State with the North, there was no need to follow the old trails to Kansas. The whole industry of cattle in Texas changed from an adventure into a real business. And one major thing was about to happen to Texas style: those same rail lines that could take the cattle out of Texas could now import goods the North had to offer, in a manner much more rapid and efficient than the tall sailing ships of the Port of Galveston. Life and lifestyle were about to change for Texas in a big way.

(Inset) *The utilitarian chuck wagon, still in use on many Texas ranches, sometimes finds itself doing new duty in backyard entertaining.*

46

CATTLE BARONS PUT IT ALL TOGETHER

There would always be the smaller cattle operations, but from this transition in transportation emerged a new fixture to this land—the cattle baron. Huge ranches consisting of hundreds of thousands of acres developed. Ranch owners who sought a life as big as the land they sprang from wanted more than an adobe with a wood-burning stove. They wanted to build empires.

These cattlemen were usually well traveled and educated. They had seen the rest of the world and wanted to bring it back to Texas. Certainly the money and the means were now in place. Their castles, though built out of indigenous raw materials, were filled with the finest wares from the East and magnificent furnishings from Europe. In a new cattle baron's style, these fittings were mixed with the traditions of the West and cowboy life to create a very unique presentation. A prized saddle might be displayed on a stand next to a Chippendale settee; a pair of spurs was thrown onto a gold-leaf server; an oil portrait of a favorite bull was hung over a Victorian sofa. Native arts and crafts also found their way into the setting—rugs, blankets, pottery, and beadwork—having the emotional appeal of souvenirs of an era that the cattle barons had watched pass and reminders of how far they and their land holdings had evolved. As upholstery became worn, it was often recovered with readily available cowhide, sometimes with the hair left right in place. In fact, the leather-upholstered couch studded with bronze or brass tacks has become classically traditional, and it seemed to have come into its own during the cattle baron years.

Cowboy craftsmen, during their time off from working with the herds, developed their own form of folk art that encompassed furnishings such as chairs, shelves, and hall trees supported by or adorned with the horns of the cattle they tended.

The cattle baron style was certainly a show of Texas expressing herself as the world expected to see her—big and bold. Not always in step with current fashion, but creating style through the mix of both the expected and the unexpected.

The most rustic and elegant of objects can be combined to create a setting that, while still formal, is comfortable and inviting.

The library at Hacienda Calhoun offers a peaceful retreat for reflecting on the written word and artifacts of a more violent time in Texas.

PATRIOTISM BLOSSOMS UNDER
THE AMERICAN FLAG

Obviously, the sixth flag to fly over Texas was the American flag, and no place could
be as American as Texas. It is a place where people have fought to be free and independent. It is a place where each group that came contributed unique tastes, arts,
and backgrounds to help mold this state into the legendary place it is today. All dis-
cussions of materials aside, it is the Texan who built Texas style in his quest to
simply be free. And to this day, it is still the Texan way to live free, building the life
one wants from the resources Texas has to offer.

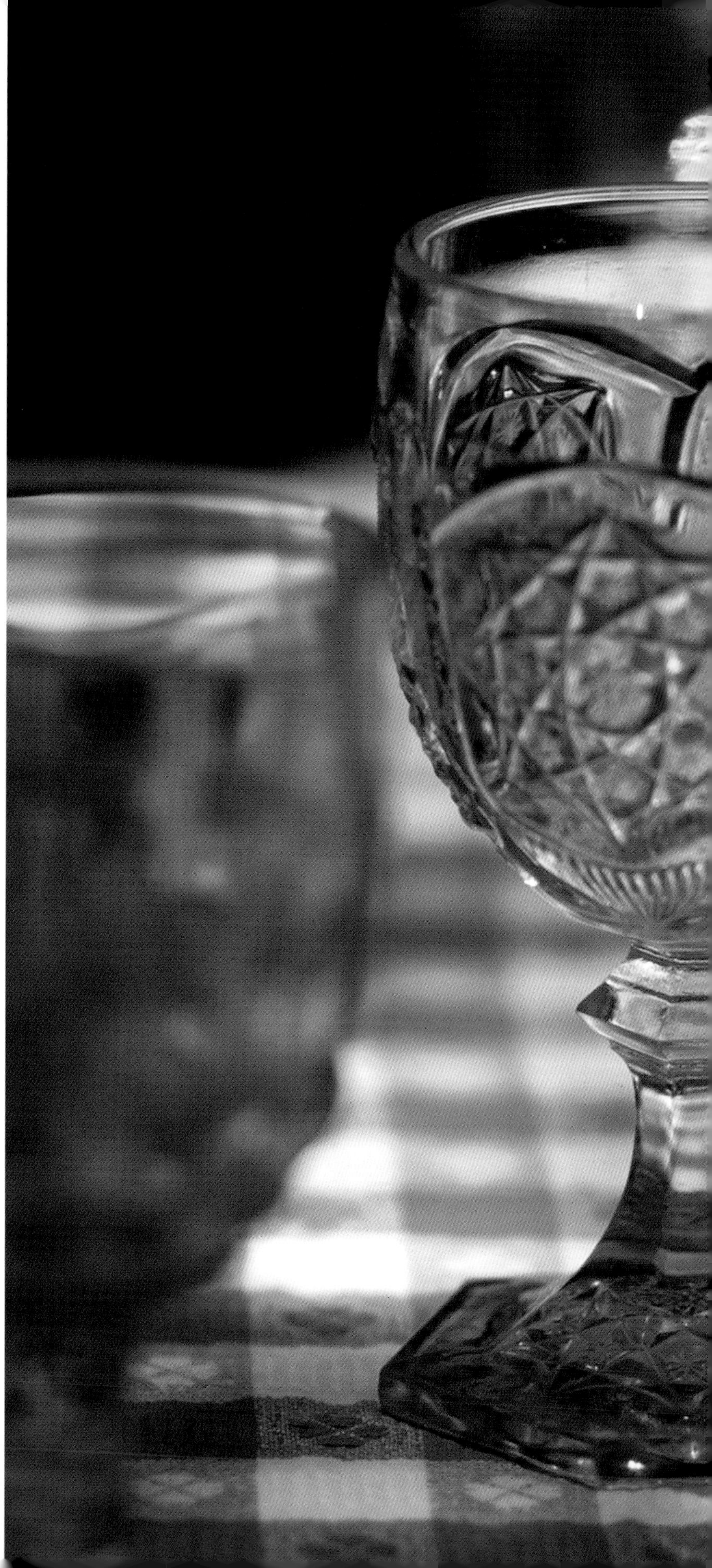

Oil's new wealth brought prosperity to many and enabled people to acquire luxuries they had only dreamed of before.

THE EXCESS OF OIL'S NEW WEALTH

The discovery of oil in Texas in the 1920s also affected Texas style. However, these changes were brought about more by the new abundance of money than by the actual presence of oil. This was a time when many an overnight millionaire tried to import to Texas much of what Texas was not meant to be, like stuffing a country girl into a couture dress: they could make the dress fit, but they could never make the girl look at home in it.

It was under this influence that the quirky and sometimes tacky aspects of Texas style were born. Texas slipped off course for a while as many folks tried to prove her to be as modern and stylish as the latest Manhattan trend.

We Texans embrace our excesses in the same way we do our restraints—with pride. "Did you hear the one about the oil man who had an optical company grind the windshield of his Cadillac to match his glasses prescription? Seems he hated having to wear his specs when he drove!" We Texans love this stuff, and can still appreciate the occasional big blond hairdo, for these things mix with the subtleties of Texas to make her unique and perpetuate her legend.

Today's Texans are just as independent as their predecessors and just as connected to the land on which they live. Even those Texans who live in metropolitan areas maintain a connection to the Texas countryside. In the most urban of Texas's settings, you are never far from a rural escape. Most Texans vacation within their own state, and many maintain second homes or retreats in the country. Some even take the leap and transplant themselves to the Texas countryside.

Texas country style today is a defiant product of the pioneer spirit that founded this state. It is a lust for freedom, space, and self-expression.

CREATING A COUNTRY STYLE
ALL YOUR OWN

You certainly don't have to be in Texas to celebrate regional and familial influences.

★ Begin a scavenger hunt with your family in the search for what makes your town, region, or state unique. Is it the architecture style of old downtown? the trees and wildflower varieties? perhaps the birds and other wildlife that frequent the parks and yards?

★ Acquaint yourself with local history. What was the impetus for the founding of your town? Is there a major industry or occupation that defines your region—mining? the railroad? farming? tourism? Imagine the clever vintage artifacts that could subtly recall and pay homage to those people who first settled your area.

(Far Left) The last reminders of ranch trucks long-since rusted away linger on a log barn. Hand-hewn log construction was common in Texas, where trees were available for building.

(Left) Most often thought of as a barren place, Texas is also a place of rivers and lakes. A collection of vintage fishing gear could become a wonderful and decorative tribute to the fisherman in your own family.

Old reels wait patiently for spring and a crisp fishing license.

✭ Bring the landscape inside your home by giving a hint of what's outside. For instance, if you live near a river, lake, or the sea, you could make attractive displays of fishing gear, river rocks, or shells. If you live in a desert region, creative displays of rocks, timeworn branches or cactus could connect your space to nature.

✭ A further reminder of your geographic region can be achieved through your choice of colors for walls and accessories. If in a desert, sand colors and pale greens will reflect what you see on a recreational drive. If near the mountains, richer greens and browns will bring that spirit into your home.

(Right) A thousand lies about the "one that got away" are contained in this few inches of shelf.

✴ Look for ways to bring the history of your area into your living space as well. Artifacts from your town or area's past are powerful ways to give your home the feeling of heritage.

✴ Choose artworks that depict local historical themes or regional landscape. The art can be excellent conversation starters for an evening of entertaining at home.

Native American arts of all kinds are not only a decorative investment but also reminders of those who first called this great state home.

57

✶ Framed vintage photos honor the progress made by those before you and connect you to their contributions in a way that is not only visually interesting but also educational. Many public libraries have photo archives that are open to the public.

✶ Seek out and collect folk art that employs natural materials from your region.

✶ Consider locally handmade furniture, either old or new.

All other elements aside, your living space should speak loudest about you and your family. Your own heritage and interests are the greatest gifts you can share as a host. Mementos and photos that have been tucked away in boxes are keeping silent the voice of your past. Share only what you wish, but share your heritage with those you invite into your home as well as with your own family. You might be surprised to see them developing an interest and pride in where and who they came from.

★ The sporting equipment you used as a youngster, and toys you or your ancestors played with are just a few candidates. You will find that beloved objects, in a way, take on and preserve the soul and spirit of people or times that have passed.

★ Tools of your family's trade can be displayed in groupings. Were your family teachers? politicians? grocers? laborers? What remnants of their work might be tucked away in closets or attics, or purchased at a thrift store? A vintage adding machine and a pile of old ledger books could remind all that your mother was a bookkeeper. A person in the business of computers might display a collection of old typewriters, the very instrument their career helped to make obsolete.

*Hammers and mallets of work and play
wait in the smithy and on the back porch.*

Texas is also a land of great nautical heritage, with ports like Galveston having once been some of the busiest in the country. Texas once even boasted its own navy!

59

★ Reminders of your family's talents and hobbies make for warm nooks and tabletop displays: A vintage sewing box with partially used skeins of thread and an embroidered pillowcase can be a nostalgic reminder of Grandmother's skillful needlework. Some carpenter's tools bring to mind a father's craftsmanship in the wood shop. A couple of prized family recipes artistically framed and hung in the kitchen vouch for an inherited love of cooking. A funny photograph and a couple of costume pieces not only tell about Aunt Thelma's amateur thespian career but might initiate some creative play.

★ Shadow boxes of photos and artifacts displayed together in an entry or hallway can help a newcomer to your home get a feeling for what you're about.

The artifacts of Texas and the West, when showcased as décor, tell a story as they enhance a space, generating a feeling of heritage and tradition.

★ Bring out your own or a family member's collection for display. If Aunt Sofie had a love for salt and pepper shakers, her efforts can delight all who enter your home.

★ What in your family background brings a nostalgic lump to your throat? Was it watching the 4th of July parade together? Vacationing with grandparents at the family cabin? Caring for a beloved family pet? Photographs or souvenirs from such events, tastefully displayed, can bind younger generations to those who have gone before.

★ A collection of the family's military pins and honors, partnered with a real flag or an artistic representation of one, speaks of your family's patriotism.

✻ In case you don't find your own family history all that interesting, you might consider compensating for a self-perceived lack of color—people do it all the time. Scour flea markets and junk shops, gathering up old photos of interesting-looking people. Set them around your home in vintage-looking frames.

For a game, the family could make up stories about the people or fabricate "memories" the picture calls to mind. Would such an innocent hoax be considered strange? Possibly no stranger than gathering around us all sorts of furnishings and accessories that bear no relation to our history or interests.

✻ Creating a rich, layered look of regional or cultural heritage will benefit by your simply slowing down. Certainly the anchor pieces of a room, such as sofas, tables and chairs, can be gathered in a short time, but leave some holes. You never know what you may run into in a week or two. And it's surprising how your own moods as a shopper from week to week can influence your choices. Spreading your choices out over a period of time will help prevent a room's being too focused on one particular texture or silhouette. An interesting room will reflect the fascinating range of your personality.

THE
IMPERIAL
DICTIONARY
VOL. III
L — SCR

elegant country living

Thinking of country living, especially in Texas, one would probably think of rough-ing it in a log cabin or toughing it out in an isolated ranch house. While this may be the case some of the time, there are also homes in even the remotest of settings that are havens for living well, eating well, and enjoying the kind of life that one might expect to find on an old-money family compound in upstate New York or Cape Cod.

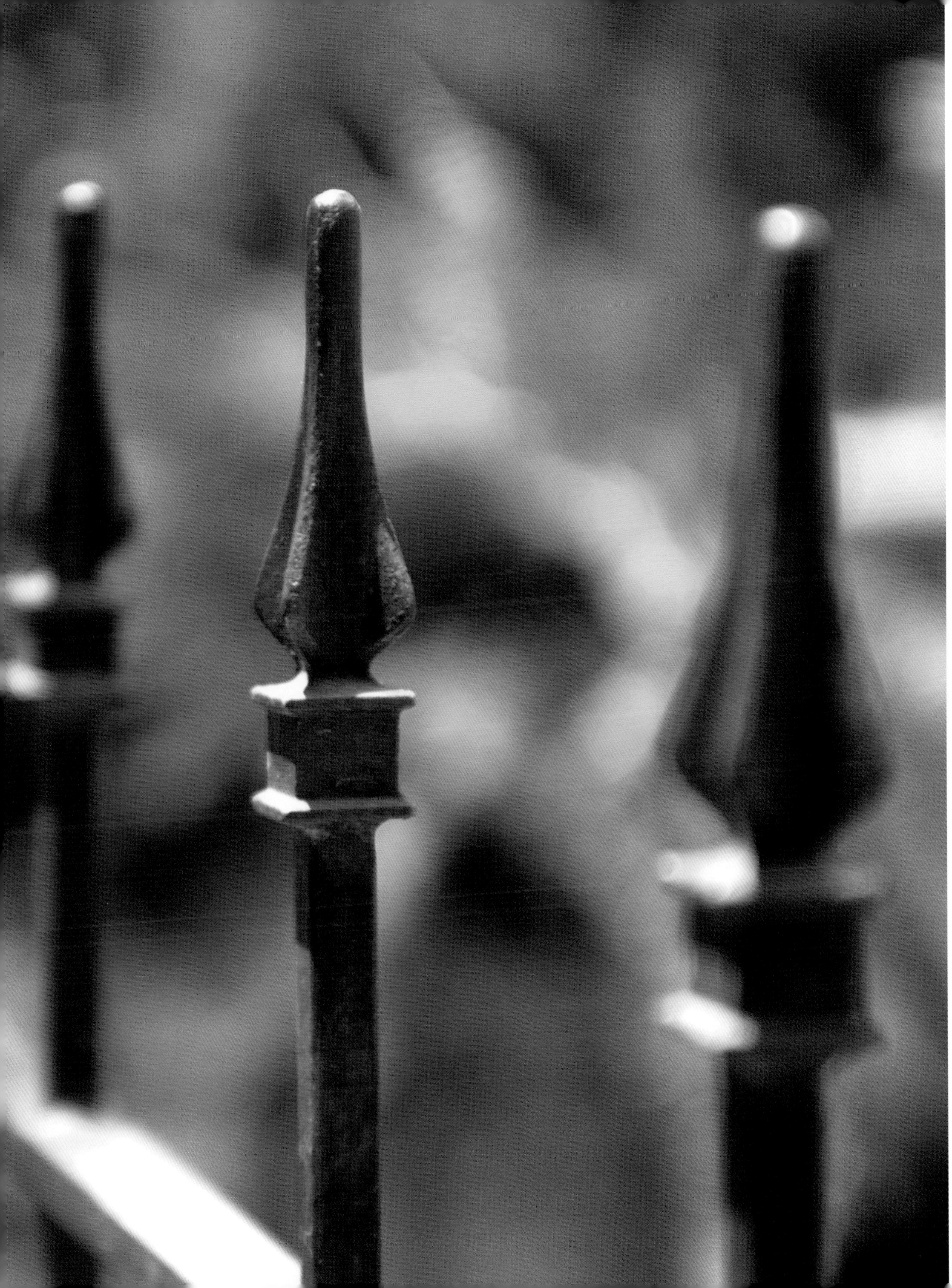

HERITAGE ELEGANCE

The term *heritage elegance* would be appropriate for the style of living that surrounds Edgewater, a family estate on the banks of the Guadalupe River near Hunt, Texas.

Edgewater began its life in 1886 as a mere hunting cabin and then expanded under the dream and passion of a retired sea captain named Regan. Captain Regan began his initial construction of the main house shortly after the turn of the century, only to see all of his efforts mercilessly washed away in a flood of the Guadalupe, which, while usually tranquil and clear, can change personalities in a heartbeat after a few days of heavy rain. But Captain Regan had weathered too many storms at sea to allow one river to stand in the way of his dream, so reconstruction began immediately.

As the evening settles, Edgewater seems to glow with life. Originally built at the turn of the twentieth century as a sea captain's rustic hunting retreat, Edgewater now stands as a symbol of one family's commitment to elegant living in the Texas country.

The cypress-lined Guadalupe River is the quintessential Texas Hill Country setting. Its waters have reflected many years of graceful living here at Edgewater.

Regan designed an amazing home along the river. The four-level mansion, built of native stone, is impressive from any angle. The highly refined woodwork and elegant hardware are reminiscent of that found within the tall sailing ships the captain had commanded. Even the layout of the home has a shipboard feeling, with windows lining galleries and various balcony levels like a ship's deck, affording nicely framed views of the river. Captain Regan built a fine place to live out his life, where he could hunt, fish, and see and touch water each day, as he had done his whole life.

Long after the captain's passing, the story of Edgewater then jumps to the 1950s, when it became a resort that could be rented for family vacations. Not a bad occupation for the old place—sending people home with postcard-like memories of summers along the Guadalupe. By this time, Edgewater had several cabins, perfectly sized and outfitted for family retreats—especially perfect for the David Burnham family. Beginning in 1957, the Burnhams vacationed at Edgewater; while David Burnham fished upstream, the kids swam downstream, each year adding memories to their souls like new charms on a bracelet. That was, until 1964 when Edgewater was put up for sale. Not surprisingly, Burnham bought Edgewater, giving his descendants a gift that lives on to this day.

Small shelves can tell big stories when properly dressed. Note how the spent matches on the match holder and the simple pinecone on the shelf add life to inanimate vignettes.

Fine European lace with silhouettes of deer connects the interior of Edgewater with the natural setting of the property. Native deer abound on the riverbanks of the Guadalupe.

David Burnham is now gone, but the Burnham family through the years have picked up the torch of Captain Regan and maintained Edgewater the way one would maintain and improve a fine sailing vessel. Stepping inside the main house, one can sense the legacy of the man who built it. Edgewater stands proud in her beautiful riverside setting. She is beautifully appointed with leather furniture contrasting with the fine European lace on the windows. Antiques of both European and American origin mix happily with an eclectic collection of western and traditional art.

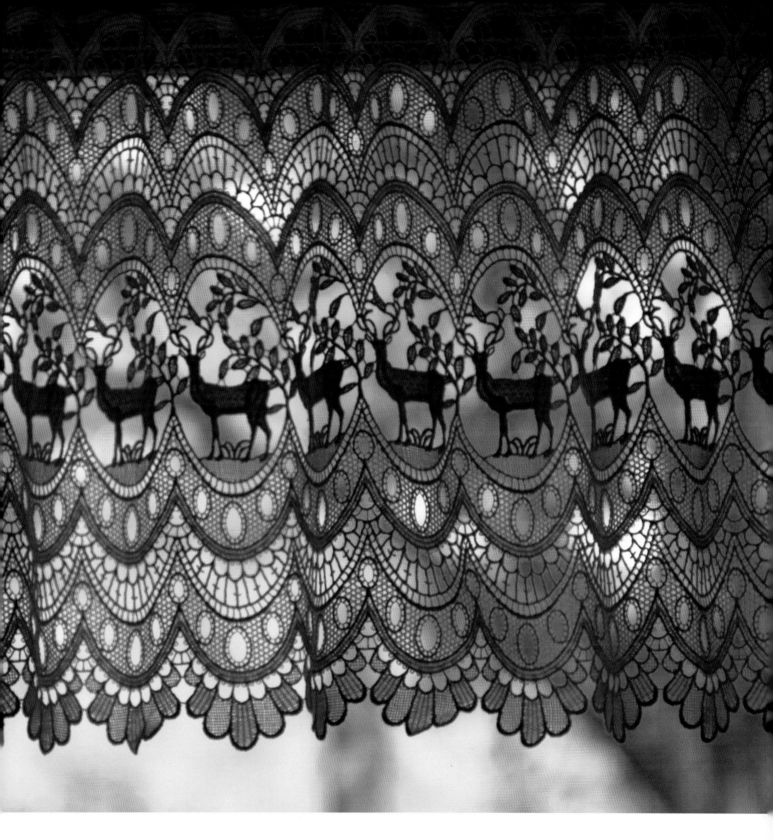

Edgewater gives the visitor the perfect presentation of heritage elegance. Fine silver stands ready to entertain while subtly rugged elements speak of the history and traditions of the Lone Star State.

The dining area is always ready to entertain, with good silver out and Mom's favorite dishes displayed on the cupboard. Shelves are filled with well-worn books and photos of the family through the years. Black-and-white images of summers past share precious memories of the Burnham family's heritage, while color photos of the next generation give us a peek into the future of this family. Even a photo of old Captain Regan astride his favorite hunting pony holds a place of prominence. One instantly feels a sense of tradition in Edgewater that is purely Texan. The décor has been accumulated rather than assembled, which gives the home a natural and comfortable feel, even though the estate setting and the living traditions there are quite formal.

The careful placement of a chair and bowl, an open book, and the random arrangement of the fruit all work together to create the illusion that someone has just walked away from the setting, giving life to the room even when no one is present.

The art of accumulation and managing clutter give hint of the property's history, location, and the interests of the family members.

In addition to the main house, the Edgewater compound includes a party house that has big, open spaces suitable for group activities, and there are additional cabins ready for each family member's return to this special place. The most interesting building—Regan's original hunting cabin—belongs to Burnham's daughter Bonnie Swinney. It is constructed of fossilized rock harvested from a nearby ranch. In addition, a pool and cookhouse occupy the center of the grounds. Another Burnham daughter, Molly, and her husband, Frank Maresh, live in the main house full time; yet, Edgewater waits ready for any of the now greatly extended Burnham family to return to her comfort and grace. In a way, it seems to wait for the return of Captain Regan, and one easily feels his presence while strolling about the property.

A croquet set waits patiently for summer on the back porch of Captain Regan's original hunting cabin, built in 1886.

(Overleaf) The fossilized stone used to construct the captain's original cabin is believed to have been harvested on the famous YO Ranch. Early photos indicate that the cabin originally had a stone roof, perhaps inspired by one of the captain's sea voyages to Ireland.

Edgewater offers its guests a traditional yet inviting and comfortable haven to let go of those things that stressful modern lives might give the illusion of importance, and puts focus back on the simple art of living well.

An umbrella rack hosts unexpected but companionable pieces, some of which tell a little about the family's interests.

In spite of Edgewater's privileged lifestyle, its occupants exhibit the grit and a "remember the Alamo" attitude that are the hallmarks of the Texas spirit. For example, when the river rose out of control once again in summer 2000, the whole lower level of the main house was submerged. Just a short time after, one of the clan reported with a slight chuckle that "we even found a fish in the stovetop, but the whole mess is already cleaned up."

Edgewater, and many other abodes like it, absorbs a little piece of the soul of all those who live and visit there, and eventually assembles these pieces into a spirit of its own that is felt the minute one walks through the door. It is not an overwhelming feeling, this spirit, but just a whisper in the ear that this old house has enjoyed the life that has gone on within it as much as those who did the living.

CREATING THE HERITAGE ELEGANCE STYLE

The elegant Texas country style can be created to suit your living space anywhere—city or country, east or west. Adapting the style can be done on many different levels. One budget-conscious alternative is to do up just one room in elegant Texas-heritage style—or with the accoutrements and artifacts of your own family's occupational heritage. Imagine a guest's delight at being transported to the American West as they sleep in your guest room or are entertained in your den, surrounded by your own collection of western art or artifacts. After all, what child has not dreamed of being a cowboy or cowgirl?

The look of heritage elegance is pleasing, warm, and not that difficult to achieve. The key factor in assembling this style of décor is in slowing down and collecting your décor over a period of time and from different sources, rather than buying everything at once. You will find that accumulated furnishings—some family heirlooms, some memorabilia of favorite ancestors and emblems of their occupations and lifestyle, some treasured purchases that really appeal to you—will allow you to *express* yourself in the style rather than just *decorating* in the style. This will give your setting the feeling of tradition that only time can create.

Let your first treasure hunt take place among the goods that you already own or that would be accessible from a relative. Remember that in the early days of Texas, people lived with what they had brought from their previous homes and then combined those with things available locally. The classic look for a retreat or cabin is generally achieved with hand-me-down furnishings from the main house in town.

Mike Mullins's 4M Ranch is a wonderful study in contemporary architecture that still retains some hints of western tradition. The use of elegant yet rustic furnishings allows the space to make a unique and powerful statement about Texas and the West.

While Mullins's kitchen is certainly state of the art, the use of beams and natural finishes helps maintain the rustic theme of the whole house.

The elements of the elegant heritage look are easily obtained and may already be in your possession.

Some tips for creating heritage elegance:

★ Flowers are always right. For heritage elegance, try arranging some varieties that Grandmother might have had in her garden.

★ Mixing in something that is unexpected will make your room interesting.

★ Setting a table with fine china is a symbol of living well, but setting it with mismatched pieces and good silver would be a creative show of free expression. Give it a try!

✱ Go soft on the upholstery. It doesn't always have to be leather; plaids can give your setting a softer elegant feel. In keeping with the heritage theme, there's many a hand-me-down Early American-style sofa tucked away in the auntie's attic that, with the right fabric, can have a grand new life in your country retreat setting.

✱ Old hooked rugs for the floors, amateur artwork on the walls, maybe even Uncle Bud's trophy deer head retrieved from the garage can all be handsomely blended into an elegant heritage setting.

Curtains that sweep the floor are more elegant than those that just skim the bottom of the window frame. And this example shows that the window treatments don't even have to match.

Fine art does not always have to be present to create a gallery effect. Here a collection of paint-by-numbers paintings is grouped by theme and displayed in a child's room.

✶ Assemble the furniture and art resources of your family first and see what you have. Picturing them all together (use snapshots, hand-drawn representations, or even just the names of the items written on a piece of paper) can help you make the selections and combinations that will speak well and interestingly of your family and where you came from. Don't be afraid to share your quirkiness either. If Cousin Sara could not control her "paint-by-numbers" hobby, then display her work proudly as a celebration of what makes your family unique.

Try to break away from the notion that all things must match to work harmoniously. Remember that hand-me-down and cast-off objects can get a second chance at life in your heritage elegance setting.

89

✹ Remember, it is the unexpected combination of objects that creates interest. Mixing some items that are traditionally formal with other items that are purely rustic can also be fun. Making such companionships work is not as tricky as it might sound. One of Texas's most fierce fighting men, Jim Bowie, is said to have always maintained quite an elegant lifestyle at home. A southerner before coming to Texas, he clung to his proper southern ways. This buckskin-clad former riverboat gambler not only knew how to use the Bowie knife (so-named for Jim's brother, a knife maker) but also knew which fork to use with each course of the meal.

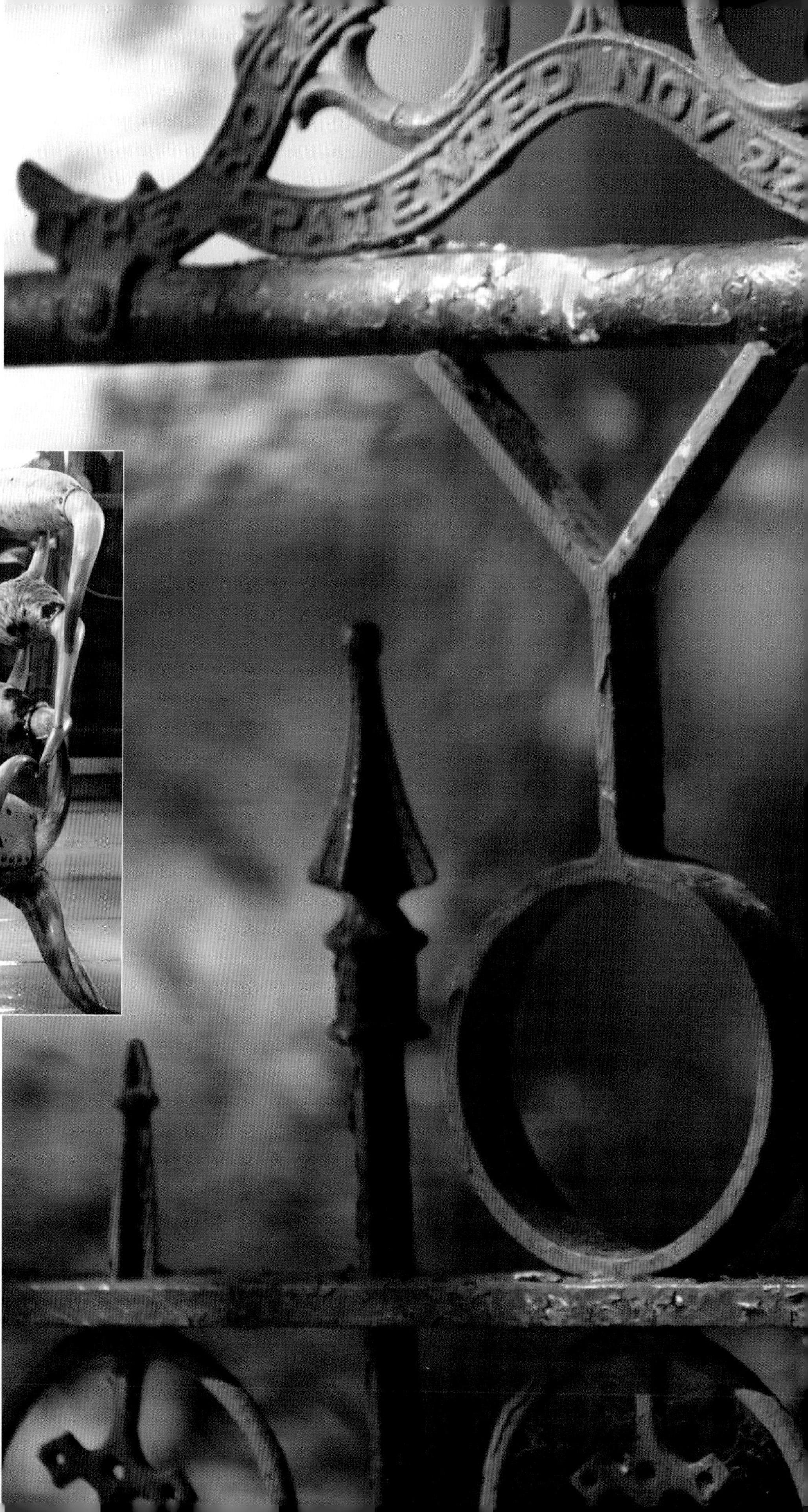
PATENTED NOV 22

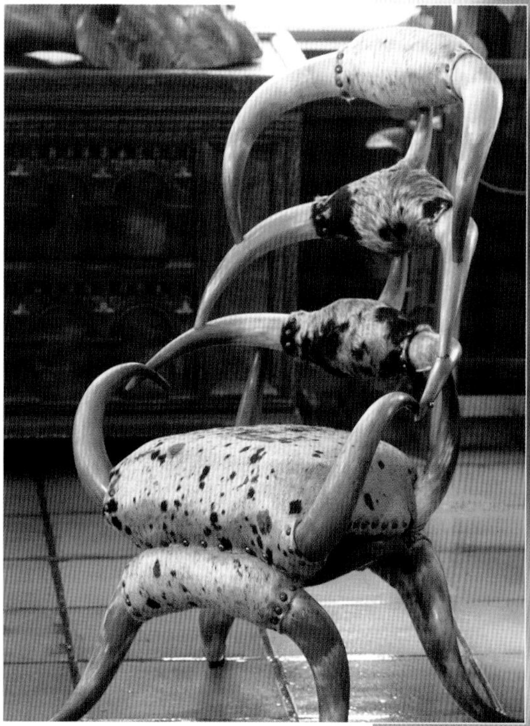

(Left) A Victorian-era steer-horn chair at the home of Walter Schreiner on the legendary YO Ranch. Even the hair-on hide used to upholster this cowboy folk art piece carries the YO brand. Both horns and hide probably grazed this famous ranch in the cattle-king era and were tended by Walter's famous ancestors.

An old ox yoke from the late 1800s finds new function as a chandelier in the ballroom of the headquarters of the YO.

CATTLE BARON ELEGANCE

The ultimate Texas look is that developed by the cattle barons. How to describe the cattle baron look? It's akin to the use of both the feminine and masculine elements of decorating. An example would be a traditional backdrop (feminine, formal, à la Victorian) for a room filled with rugged furnishings and collections (masculine, such as leather, rough-finish woods, cowboy gear). In other words, finding the perfect balance between leather and lace, allowing the two contrasting elements to coexist perfectly.

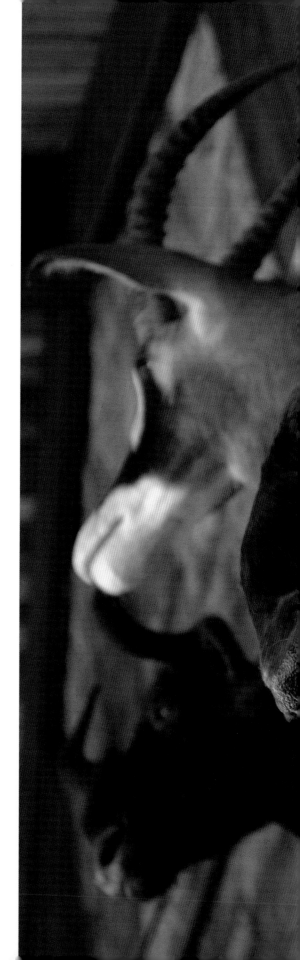

(Inset) This chandelier, more than ten feet in height, in the ballroom of the YO Ranch headquarters is adorned with the branding irons of dozens of famous ranches.

The home of Walter Schreiner on the famous YO is probably one of the most perfect examples of the true cattle baron style of living. All of the fineries the world has to offer mix so well with the rugged elements of the frontier. Beauty in such a harsh landscape seems magnified, and the effect is stunning.

Achieving this look is not as complicated as it may sound, but it should always lean toward the masculine influence, using formal touches to tone things down a bit.

A rich example of this style is the home of Walter Schreiner on the famous YO Ranch in Mountain Home, Texas. Founded in 1880 and maintained by the Schreiner family ever since, the ranch covers some 40,000 acres. This home is a perfect mix of elegance and cattleman's heritage. Fine European furniture is right at home with massive western paintings. The formal dining area is equipped with the best china, crystal, and silver but is lit by a chandelier of antlers. A grand piano sits in the shadow of classic works of taxidermy.

Photos and artifacts of the Schreiner family are tastefully disbursed throughout the home, reminding one that the elegant lifestyle at this ranch goes beyond cattle and land; it is about the people who have built and maintained this empire known as YO.

Many collections are grouped throughout the home. A library holds artworks in oil, photography, and bronze as well as artifacts, while a collection of cowboy and Native American trappings is displayed beyond the library, creating visual interest in the other areas of the home used for entertaining. Guests are immediately aware, though, that they are not in a museum but amidst rich family tradition.

CREATING THE CATTLE BARON ELEGANCE STYLE

This cattle baron style of decorating need not be limited to those lucky enough to live the ranching life. It creates an ideal atmosphere for a home or professional office. If you have a personal collection of western art or your family shares this love of the West together, what better way to celebrate this than by assembling your collection as a family project?

Some tips for creating cattle baron elegance:

★ In woods, stay away from the lighter oaks, which are more casual in feel. Choose either from the refined finish of the darker hardwoods or choose pine; pine is abundant in Texas and has been utilized by every generation.

(Far left) This credenza and top cabinet, offered by Antèks Home Furnishings of Dallas, could provide the cattleman the perfect place to review his "tally" books, or could be just the spot to tackle the finances of a modern-day household.

Using heirloom rugs has always been a sign of good breeding and elegance. Combine that with several pieces of simply designed furniture and your room will make a statement that says elegant taste all the way.

The cattle baron look is a mixture of art, artifacts, and Victorian silhouettes, letting the masculine prevail while the feminine elements of Victorian design are used to provide contrast, thus creating an environment that provides visual interest by exploiting the friendly competition of these themes.

★ For the floors, Navajo weavings or kilim rugs having a Navajo feel are good choices. A spotted cowhide can cover floor space as well, and again, don't be afraid of reaching toward Victorian designs in floor coverings. The western look will start taking shape as you blend all of these elements.

★ Combine throw pillows of both leather and fringed fabric, even velvet.

★ If you want to soften the leather or feminize the balance in your décor, fabric is the key. Surround a leather sofa or pile a bed with pillows, blankets or throws. Or choose an upholstery option of leather combined with a kilim or a tapestry that might have hints of Native American design.

(Far left) The cattle baron look is softened toward the feminine by the use of pillows and patterned fabrics.

(Below) Here, a tapestry is hung as the backdrop to a rustic dining corner. Combined with fine crystal and linens, western-theme china ties the table setting to the cattleman's world.

✱ If you are decorating living space, pick your sofa first—and go with leather. Perhaps add an easy chair with ottoman. Leather is classic and can live among many other décor styles should you find yourself tiring of your cattle baron status later.

✱ As you select furniture, try using Victorian silhouettes.

✱ For lighting, you could spring for an antler light fixture, but if this is not in the budget, keep the overhead lighting and sconces, if used, formal in style. For your lower lighting, have some fun by combining antique table lamps with rawhide or cowhide lamp shades. Lamps found at garage sales or flea markets can save you some money for more-expensive shades. A fringed Victorian shade will make the cattle baron statement just as loudly as will rawhide.

★ For wall treatments, work with anything from plain white paint to busy Victorian wallpaper, but selecting earth-tone paint colors will be more in keeping with the Texas spirit of acknowledging the natural setting of the home.

★ Western art and vintage photographs, as well as Native American, cowboy, or Victorian artifacts, all tie in with the cattle baron style.

Once you have created the backdrop, enjoy the collecting—and make it personal. Fill the room with furniture, textures, and fabrics that speak to your personal concept of what the West is.

The art of living well in the country is just that—an art. In Texas it has common elements, but it takes as many forms as there are people who pursue this lifestyle.

★ Whatever your western collecting passion is, there's a way to display your treasures to enhance your environment.

FROM TEXAS SAFARI

TO ULTIMATE ESCAPE

rustic country living

Rustic living in the Texas countryside can be as tame or as wild as one wants it to be. This is where independence and free choice really come into play. Retreat styles range from simple log buildings with minimal amenities to fully outfitted Texas safari-style dwellings.

Texas has changed through the years in response to the simple evolution of the world around her. Oil prices have slowed the once unstoppable business of crude, and the cost of raising a calf to the point of it being beef on hoof is almost a break-even affair. Texas now looks to high-tech as her new business frontier, with entrepreneurial pioneers leading the way.

There is no artist who could paint a finer backdrop for the rustic lifestyle than the Texas countryside. It provides not only the setting for this choice in living but also the inspiration for those who make the commitment to rustic living.

The Texas longhorn did his job well in the late 1800s to make the beef industry a permanent part of the Texas landscape. But as years passed and the beef market became more particular, the rangy old longhorn yielded just too tough a cut of meat in comparison to the imported breeds of cattle developed specifically to produce a marbleized and tender steak or roast. The very things that made the longhorn the perfect beef animal of his day—his strength and toughness that enabled him to be driven all the way to Kansas—were to be his downfall as tastes and options changed. The longhorn almost became extinct. Today he is making a comeback, partly out of sentimentality for the debt we owe this old pioneer of the industry, and partly in expectation that, in a health-conscious marketplace, the demand for leaner cuts of meat may move him back to a more popular position. But many Texans raise longhorns simply to admire the homely yet stately animal that is a readily recognized symbol for the state of Texas.

Some ranchers have turned a new direction and are keeping the tradition alive in a most unusual way and with profitable results: African game ranching has come to Texas.

The ranching heritage of Texas has evolved in a direction never dreamed of by early cattlemen such as Captain King (founder of the largest cattle ranch in Texas, still in operation) and Charlie Goodnight. This view of central Texas might well be mistaken for the Serenghetti.

TEXAS SAFARI

Remember the idea mentioned earlier, of delighting the eye by mixing in the unexpected? Who would have expected to find African wildebeests, zebra, or even water buffalo grazing alongside a Texas longhorn in his own pasture? These strange bedfellows make up the new breed of ranching.

Pony Creek Ranch, owned and operated by Jim Berry, is no dude ranch. It is a homestead devoted to the business of raising exotic game. Berry and ranchers like him breed and raise exotic stock to supply other such operations and preserves all around the country. You do not have to look far on this property to see Jim's love of Africa; it is on hoof and wandering everywhere. This rocky yet grassy area of Texas near the Paluxy River even offers a backdrop that mimics parts of Africa, and it is easy at times to feel as though you have been swept to another continent.

Pony Creek Ranch, near Glen Rose, is a perfect example of rustic living—Texas style. It is, however, a working ranch, and beyond the gate of this courtyard are fences to ride and livestock to tend.

(Inset) The headquarters of Pony Creek Ranch is actually a collection of structures artfully joined to work in unison as a beautiful home, built around an old homestead that was original to the place.

The main headquarters of Pony Creek Ranch was in a state of ruin when Berry took it over. Most people would have seen the old ranch house as nothing more than a source for weathered wood. But Jim's strong Texas spirit couldn't let this old place down; he set about giving it a new life not only as a working ranch but also as a place to spend quality time with his children and the lucky friends who get to visit.

While the well-planned guest accommodations make visitors to Pony Creek Ranch feel like they are at a rustic resort, there are plenty of reminders that they are on a working ranch.

Yet, back at the headquarters of the ranch, once one moves beyond the architectural impact of this dwelling, the combinations of décor are both surprising and appealing. An adobe courtyard leads one past a huge outdoor cooking area, past racks of saddles and working gear, to the entrance to a great room that was added onto the rear of the house—a room so large that a twelve-foot-diameter vintage windmill head acts as the ceiling fan overhead! This room is so grand that two small one-room antique log cabins were reconstructed within it—one to act as a card room, the other to act as Jim's office. The interior style of the ranch house starts as pure Texas ranch—with trappings of the cowboy trade on display throughout. These items are tastefully combined with African folk art and artifacts that mix with cowboy gear surprisingly well. A massive fireplace fronted by several groups of seating makes entertaining easy, as multiple accumulations of guests can form and move among different chat groups throughout the evening when Pony Creek Ranch entertains.

Native cedar vigas harvested right on the property let just enough of the sun's warmth filter through on this Texas afternoon.

A supply of brightly painted pitching washers hangs ready for the friendly yet competitive evening games at Pony Creek. After stock have been tended, fences checked, and horses and four-wheelers put to bed, the cowboy fun begins.

(Left) Many architectural elements of the Pony Creek headquarters were salvaged in the area. Some fittings, however, have been brought from as far away as Mexico.

This dogtrot between two of the guest cabins creates a perfect outdoor den for visitors to meet and enjoy conversation, which must pause on occasion for the unexpected opinion of a howling coyote.

The card room at Pony Creek Ranch is actually a small log structure that was dismantled and reassembled within the great room.

The Mike Mullins 4M Ranch brings sophistication into the cattle country of Texas with a tasteful blending of contemporary western art and fine furnishings of a type that are not always expected in ranch country.

A huge commercial kitchen occupies one corner of this great room, and a full bar fills the opposite corner. The dining room is very rustic yet formally arranged. A bunkhouse-style bedroom off the kitchen provides Jim's son with plenty of room to bring a crew of friends out to the ranch for the weekends. Another bedroom is in a loft above a small study. Other fixtures within the main house are a shuffleboard and billiards area.

An evening of fine dining and artful conversation enjoyed at the main house of Pony Creek Ranch makes one embrace the lack of diversion and sit tight for the next Texan's tall tale.

The click of the balls mingles with the jingle of spurs and the rowdy talk of cowhands glad to be done with the day's chores here in Pony Creek's billiards area.

Horses and livestock graze alongside newer immigrants to the Texas ranching landscape. As many cattle operations turn toward exotic game, a new future of ranching often wears stripes rather than the traditional spots of the Texas longhorn.

Beyond the main house, even more fun begins, in guest cabins that stand ready for friends who come out to partake in some cowboy R and R. Each cabin is unique and original; even an old stone cistern is used as guest space. The cabins are only a few steps from a swimming pool that was built to look as if it were a natural formation on the property. A stable of off-road vehicles allows visitors to roam the 1,500-acre property and admire native deer, turkeys, and a group of Texas longhorns from the famous King Ranch, all sharing space with cape buffalo, oryx, water buffalo, and a wide range of other African stock. A large herd of zebra that Jim refers to as "the kids' college fund" has been a project shared by Jim and his children, who are constantly adding to the menagerie and cultivating growth within the herd.

The Brazos River cuts a winding path through the Palo Pinto country of Texas. It is here that legendary cattleman Charles Goodnight began an empire that would later prove to be the inspiration for Larry McMurtry's Lonesome Dove.

RUSTIC RETREAT

Rocky Top Ranch, the cowboy hideaway of Ron and Deborah Hall, is the perfect example of weekending in the country. By 5:30 each Friday, the Halls are driving as quickly as they can into the Texas sunset, heading for the peace they have created in their own cowboy heaven in Palo Pinto County in the north-central region of the state, legendary land of cattleman Charlie Goodnight, who began the true industry of ranching in Texas.

The area around Palo Pinto County is a land of both beauty and history. Goodnight was the first to take on the wilderness and drive cattle herds north to Kansas, thus founding the famous Goodnight Trail. History aside, this is a beautiful part of Texas. The Brazos River cuts through rugged, sometimes mountainous and rocky terrain, with valleys of hay fields scattered along the crooks of the river's course. High rocky bluffs along the Brazos are a testament to the river's patience.

From a vantage point more than 400 feet above the Brazos River, one may sometimes find oneself taking morning coffee in the company of one of the many bald eagles that nest below.

124

Ron and Deborah are part of a generation of Americans who spent Saturday mornings glued to the television, watching Roy Rogers and Dale Evans live out every child's dream of life in the West. Ron and Deborah had to grow up, as we all must, and Ron became a dealer in fine art. The Halls, however, never relinquished those Saturday-morning cowboy dreams. Finally, when they found this bluff overlooking the Brazos, they decided to make those dreams three-dimensional, and now, their retreat sits 450 feet above the river's surface. Out back, one experiences a breathtaking view of the Brazos winding along below and maybe catches a glimpse of the bald eagles that winter here.

Childhood fans of everybody's hero, Roy Rogers, Ron and Deborah Hall built this retreat in the "New West" style of the 1940s singing-cowboy movies.

As you wind up the hill toward the Halls' house, you pass a rock whose hand-painted lettering congratulates you on successfully following Ron's map to the location. After that, you begin to feel as if you slipped through some window of time and are driving onto a 1940s movie set for a Roy Rogers or Gene Autry feature. Walking past the tack shed, you circle around a chuck wagon all set up for the night's cookout, and then you arrive at the front of the house, unabashedly western with a retro twist. They nailed it! The only thing missing is the wood-sided station wagon parked in front.

An authentic wagon wheel serves as the frame for an upstairs bedroom window.

Cowboy kitsch was often a young baby boomer's first notion of an imaginary West of brightly painted cactus and bucking broncos in silhouette. Many of those boomers, though now tied to professional obligations, seek out the "real" West as a place to test their salt against a standard that is truer than that of the corporate jungle.

128

The house is constructed of local stone whose reddish hue contrasts well with the cedar poles and timber used in the woodwork. The first architectural feature to grab your attention is the authentic wagon wheel that frames an upstairs window.

One steps inside to a paradise of western kitsch. The Halls raise longhorn cattle and are team ropers. They have carefully assembled a balanced mix of both serious and whimsical western décor.

The architecture of the interior is reminiscent of a Wyoming lodge, immediately drawing one's attention to the large great room that features beamed structure work above and a mezzanine-style balcony accessing two of the bedrooms. A massive fireplace is positioned opposite a kitchen that is fit for any ranch cook, with plenty of workspace and a long, inviting dining table. Cedar and pine are used artfully throughout the home, giving a vintage glow that perfectly showcases the Halls' incredible western collectibles.

Collections of vintage hats and boots are grouped throughout the main living area right along with the working gear the Halls use in their day-to-day ranching. Long-silent cap pistols that once fired over the handlebars of Schwinn bicycles now hang in their fancy holsters from pegs, hat racks, and hooks everywhere. A marvelous collection of both amateur and serious western art mixes well with vintage movie posters and old saddles.

The Halls have also brought together a classy collection of western lighting, both vintage and retro lighting that spreads ambiance throughout the home. Some of the lamps have transparent photographic shades showing round-up scenes and western landscapes; others have burlap shades and funky western bases.

A collection of western-hero lunch boxes graces the top of an old Hoosier cabinet, reminding us of the days when carrying lunch to school was also a way of declaring allegiance to Roy, Gene, or Hoppy. A hutch near the dining area displays a gold mine of vintage western dishes, saltshakers, and all descriptions of western bric-a-brac.

It is hard not to feel that old Saturday-morning excitement of sitting on the edge of the couch, watching Roy and Dale ride the range, and trying to ignore your mom's calls to weekend chores. These collectible cowboy kitsch items provide a wonderful means to interpret the West as many of us might wish it were.

The rustic-looking kitchen of the Halls' Rocky Top Ranch is outfitted with the best industrial-quality appliances. It's almost enough to tempt any ranch "cookie" away from his or her chuck wagon or Dutch oven.

*The western whimsy of ranch oak furniture
is reminiscent of many an old Route 66
motel. The photographic lampshade is a
1940s classic, illuminating a wonderful
piece of amateur western art.*

The furnishings are a wonderful assortment of vintage and antique pieces that bespeak 1940s western revival. There is a wide range of Ranch Oak items, readily recognizable by the use of wagon-wheel and ox-yoke shapes in both design and construction. This style of furniture saw much commercial use, with many a Route 66 motel room decked out in full western regalia.

Tramp art, which is folk art furniture built by hobbyists around the turn if the century from discarded materials and also made and sold by the hobos of the 1930s, is displayed throughout. The home also includes some Thomas Molesworth–style furniture, which utilizes the natural shapes and forms of the wood, allowing the function of the piece to work around what nature has provided in odd shapes and burls. The bedrooms feature vintage beds in the western style, with chenille and embroidered bedspreads that once covered little buckaroos as they dreamed of riding the range. One bedroom is more feminine and creates a shrine to the cowgirl with vintage photos and art.

The Halls have embraced their childhood love of the west and have found a way to connect it with their "grown-up" obligations. Five days of the week they take care of business in town, but when the whistle blows on Friday, they head west as fast as the speed limit will allow.

A place devoted to the true art of living: the LD3 Ranch of Lewis Dickson.

ULTIMATE ESCAPE

One day Lewis Dickson pushed himself away from the table—not literally, but figuratively away from a table that many would have been happy to sit at. With a successful law partnership and the excitement of living in Houston, one of the nation's largest cities, Dickson's life would have appeared enviable to those on the outside looking in. But as he sat there in his office, he decided that all that was glittering in his life was not gold, and it was time for a change. You know the feeling; many of us have the same sorts of notions, but few of us do anything about it. Lewis did. Like Papillon escaping from Devil's Island, he broke out and ran away, and once he had cleared the fence, he never looked back.

Phone conversations with Lewis seemed normal enough. He had the typical Texas accent, and everything in his demeanor was very businesslike. Finally a date was set for a visit to his ranch, and I received a very complex set of directions to his place, LD3 Ranch. On the appointed day, Marty and I followed Lewis's specific instructions, resetting the odometer here and there, looking for a high school that signaled a turn, and finally turning in "just before the metal guard rail" somewhere near New Braunfels. We slowly navigated the narrow winding road that climbed through quintessential Texas Hill Country. After crossing a ravine that has to be impassable in the slightest rainstorm, we finally began to see signs of life, but not the life we were expecting to find on that hill.

The cut stone and beam construction of Lewis Dickson's farm is a European main-stay brought to Texas by early German settlers.

The corral of the LD3, with its carnival lights strung above, is the perfect place to throw a cowboy dance. That is, unless it's time to gather in the horses.

To our right lay a vineyard straight from the French countryside, with strange big stone cisterns standing guard; directly ahead stood a log cabin so authentic looking that we wondered if it was a restored original. Carnival lights of all colors were strung over the corral.

Out from a stone barn emerged Lewis Dickson, wearing a Lacoste T-shirt and Levi's tucked into a pair of cowboy boots, the tops of which were adorned with dancing skeletons reminiscent of the Day of the Dead art typical in Mexico. He wore some sort of hipster sunglasses, and his long brown hair waved along with his stride. Running around to my side of the truck, he was almost through the window before I could get it rolled all the way down. "Are you Alan? I'm Lewis, hey." The attorney image of my imagination headed straight into the wastebasket! I had met Lewis Dickson.

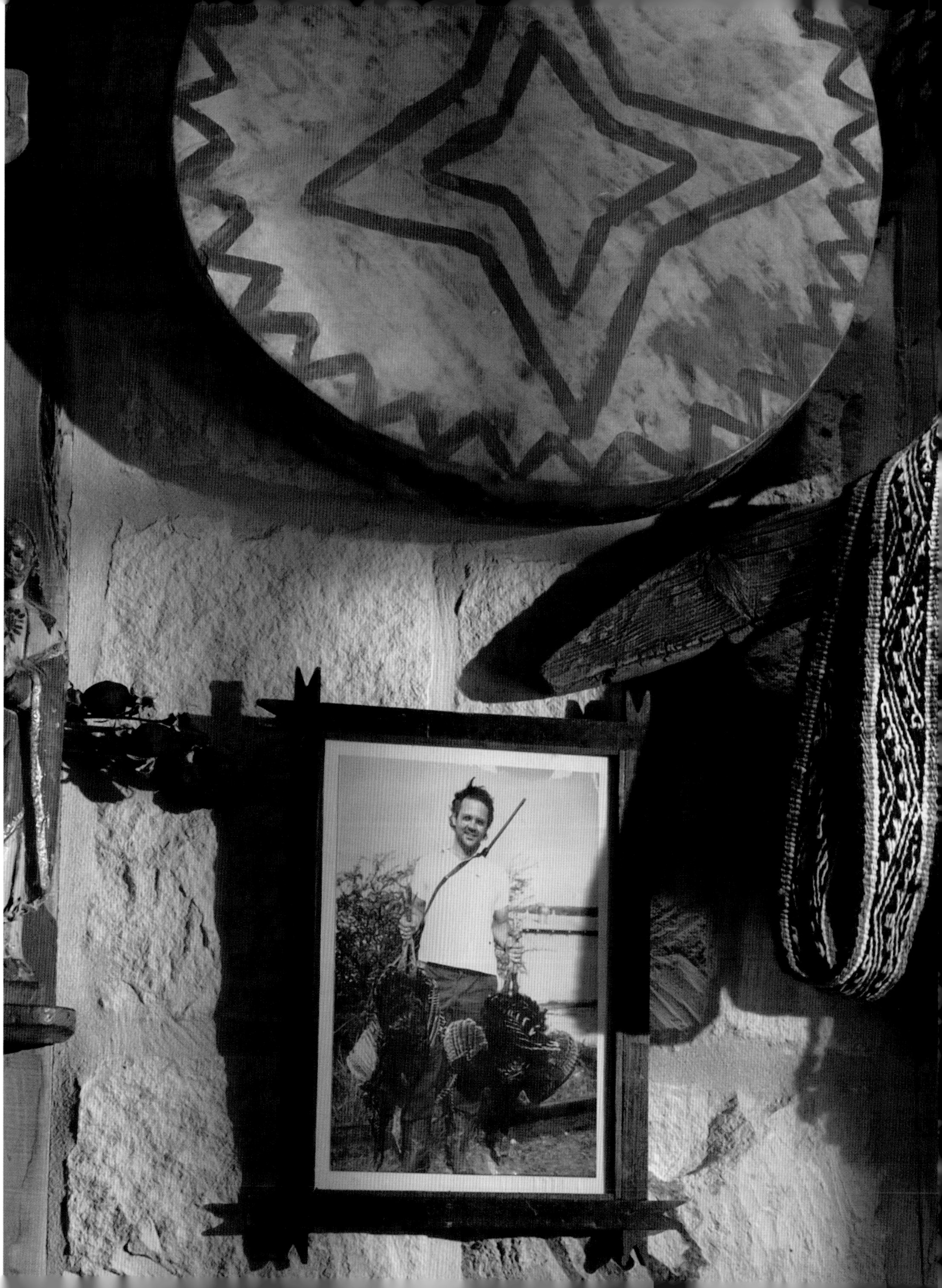

Lewis Dickson's office is unusual enough due to its location in the barn, but it also houses an amazing collection of Mexican folk art and the mementos of this sixth-generation Texan's colorful life.

Art connected to the Mexican Day of the Dead is often misunderstood. While it appears macabre, it is created in loving tribute to those who have passed before, often demonstrating a favorite passion of the deceased.

Dickson's collection contains some groupings of objects that on the surface might not seem to have a connection, but when assembled, they tell a story that Lewis himself has created.

These grape vines are the passion of Lewis Dickson.

The log home of the LD3 Ranch is made of materials harvested from the very land on which it was built. It was constructed using all original methods and many vintage tools. The separate bathroom is seen to the far right.

Out of the car, Lewis suddenly got hold of me and we were off on a tour to figure out where to get started. On our first sweep I was barraged by everything from paint horses to restored Triumph motorcycles; a log cabin with no bathroom, but a kitchen that would please any master chef; rooms filled with cowboy furniture and Mexican antiques; an office filled with incredible Mexican folk art and cowboy collectibles; paintings and serious photography covering the walls. It is a wild, Bohemian mix of everything that is cool: Texas ranch meets SoHo. As Lewis showed us his office, he opened a door to the back room and said, "This is just a place to throw crap that I'm not using right now." I peeked into the storage room to find part of Lewis's wine collection growing out from every corner across the floor, and on one suspended metal bar hung a dozen tailored suits fit for any downtown lawyer, each wearing an ever-so-slight layer of dust along the shoulders, like rusty suits of armor with no more battles to pursue.

This authentically styled outbuilding keeps the washer and dryer hidden from view.

Pretty much everything Lewis and his carpenters used to build the house and out-buildings was harvested from that ranch. The log house was hand hewn, and everything was built in the old methods, in many cases with vintage tools pulled out of retirement because they were the only ones that could do the job.

Lewis developed a fascination with grapes while in the wine country of France, such a fascination that his tidy vineyard is the model of perfection, with its own experimental watering system. And that's where the cisterns come in: they gather rainwater from the barn roof to feed the whole thing. The vine rails are covered with clothespins holding sticky-notes straight from an office desk to catch samples of marauding insects on their sticky edges. Lewis grabs one of the little yellow flags and seems to know the bug now trying to free itself from the gummy mess. "Aha!" he says in recognition, and then sticks the paper and bug into his pocket. "Over there, I'm gonna put in about forty more acres of vines, once I figure all of this out," Lewis remarks as he gestures out across part of his acreage.

Trying to get the whole way of life at LD3 in perspective, a comparison came to mind: I used to think that an Amish man had buttons on his pants only because that was the old-fashioned way of doing things. That was until I spent some time with an Amish man, who explained to me that the extra bit of effort it took him to button his pants, rather than zip them, gave him a few more seconds of time to slow down and appreciate his day. That is the only way I can describe the reason why Lewis decided on the outhouse over indoor plumbing. However, I am not talking about a privy here. This outhouse is beautiful, filled with vintage fixtures and a claw-foot tub. Any Beverly Hills matron could happily lounge the day away in there. Each step of the way from cabin to bathroom, like a button on the Amish man's pants, slows you down a bit, helping you to realize that we all live among beauty that can only be distinguished at a lower rpm.

In the kitchen is where Lewis Dickson seems to be the happiest. Whether sitting at the table for a chat or calling up his skills as master chef to feed a group of friends, this is where the former lawyer now holds court.

Considering all of the different nourishment with which Lewis feeds his soul, good food seems to be the primary fuel. His kitchen, though primitive, has the feel of a wizard's laboratory—herbs dried on hooks and nails here and there, homemade pasta hung on tree twigs suspended between old Mexican chairs, counter space absorbed by bottles of every conceivable type of oil and spice. Pots and pans hang every-where—not the shiny decorative kind, but ones that are all beat up and used well. Mixing bowls, stacks of dishes and utensils are piled everywhere. Nothing matches, but all work together. The only running water in the house is found here at the industrial-type kitchen sink. A 1940s gas stove stands in the corner; outside, a huge beehive-style stone pizza oven is fired by mesquite wood; a coffee machine that makes only one cup at a time stands ready. Nothing on its own makes total sense; but as a whole, everything provides a war chest for the chef.

Dixon is passionate about art in many varieties and surrounds himself with all kinds of visual stimulation. It's hard to get bored in this room.

Lewis's second fuel is art. He surrounds himself with all mediums of visual stimulation, from work in oils and photography to what seems to be his favorite muse, folk art. Many Mexican pieces have been assembled to provide a stark ethnic statement alongside his collection of cowboy trappings and western artifacts. Lewis's home has a gallery-like feel, with surprises for the eyes in every corner.

Lewis's new life could be described as a gallery, but not one with ropes to hold you back from what is beautiful. It is a gallery dedicated to slowing down and appreciating the finer things this world has to offer, both complex and simple. Lewis Dickson, while different, is not unique. Go to any part of the country and find people like him who are not afraid to "get off of the bus at a different stop." Not all of us can do that, but we can all lean out of the window as it pulls away from the bus stop and yell to those who have the courage to get off, "Hey, way to go! Maybe I'll get off of this thing someday too!"

In conversation while he packed up his photography equipment, Marty revealed to Lewis that he had never spent time in Texas Hill Country but thought it surely was a pretty place. Sixth-generation-Texan Lewis responded with, "You know, Marty, when Davy Crockett traveled through here on his way to the Alamo, he wrote a letter home saying that this was God's country." Marty made eye contact with me and bowed a silent "touché."

It was after dark as we made our way back down Lewis's rocky road. We pulled back onto the main highway and I gave my old truck the gas. After a few miles Marty finally broke the silence, "Man, that guy was having way too much fun!"

Rustic living in the Texas countryside is what people decide to make of it. Mainly, it seems to be all about letting go of things we thought we needed and finding out about what we really needed, to start with. Country living embraces a close connection to the land. It begins with giving ourselves this freedom to dream and realizing what we want from life, then taking some step toward it, however small. And that is, after all, the Texas way.

CREATING THE RUSTIC STYLE

Collecting and decorating with rustic furniture is like coloring outside the lines.
It's freeing and creative. Things don't have to match. And if you choose your pieces
carefully, your own use and abuse will only add to their patina.

✱ If you are bringing this look into a contemporary dwelling, try using a pale yellow or adobe color on the walls.

✱ Wood floors will give your rustic setting a natural feeling and glow. You need not be locked into hardwood; heart pine planks and other rough-looking woods can also make good flooring. Tile floors in earth-tone hues will work as well. The main idea is to connect the inside with the outdoors and nature.

✱ Think about the color plan for your project. Many times a surprising color can give a special "pop" to the setting. Perhaps it plays a supporting role rather than the lead.

Not all things need to be polished and perfect to be considered beautiful. Age and patina have beauty all their own.

★ The simple, straight lines found in most primitive furnishings are aesthetically pleasing, and the simplicity of these pieces allows you more freedom in accessorizing your space.

★ Most importantly, when shopping for original rustic furnishings, be sure the items function the way you need them to. You will come across many old pieces of furniture that look great but maybe are not structurally sound enough for day-to-day use. Do doors open and close properly? Are the drawers working properly? Do tables wobble, and can they support the weight you need them to? Always look for signs of rot or infestation in the wood. If you are inclined toward the do-it-yourself approach, you may choose to save some money by buying pieces that you can repair yourself.

There are many resources for newly constructed furnishings that offer modern
functionality while maintaining rustic
silhouettes.

✱ Look for original painted finishes that show
wear, not abuse. In these finishes you will many
times find hues that just cannot be duplicated
in today's paints.

✱ A simple coat of clear paste wax will bring the finish on old wood
back to life. Maintain your primitive furniture with an occasional wipe-
down of orange or lemon oil. You will find dealers in most antiques
markets who specialize in rustic and primitive furniture that has been
created for normal use.

Selecting anchor upholstery pieces should be the first part of any room-decorating project.

153

Two photos courtesy of Antèks Home Furnishings, Atlanta.

✶ Search out local craftspeople who produce twig or willow furniture made from indigenous branches. Willow is an excellent choice for coffee tables, side tables, writing desks, and chairs. Cushions will make twig furnishings comfy for sitting.

✶ Obviously, there is no such thing as an antique entertainment center or computer center, but you will find contemporary pieces that are constructed from old or distressed materials and many times with rubbed paint finishes that simulate years of use.

✶ Beds: most of the vintage variety will be twin or full-sized. As long as they are very sturdy, these will work great in the kids' rooms or a guest room. However, if you need a queen or king-sized bed, you should search out contemporary pieces that carry rustic flair, or find a craftsperson who can build a bed just for you.

★ You will find that leaning toward the feminine in upholstery can soften the rustic feel, giving a sense of comfort to an otherwise rough setting.

★ Plan your upholstery around the story you are trying to tell with the room. Leather is compatible with western and lodge settings, while fabrics lend a cheerful ambience in cabin or country applications. Don't be afraid of using tasteful floral patterns.

★ When planning floor coverings, choose from Native American or vintage hooked rugs. If these are not available, rag rugs and contemporary hooked rugs are available in a variety of themes and colors.

Western-theme accessories come in a variety of rustic styles. Here are cowboys and horses in a variety of colors and vintages.

155

★ Lighting in a rustic room should be kept at a low level with table lamps and sconces. The overhead lighting fixtures could be of antler or forged iron construction and wired to dimmers for controlling the brightness. If you keep the light at a low level, your space can have the warm glow of a make-believe cabin in the woods. Have fun with whimsical lamps that have outdoor themes, such as fishing and wildlife. Forged iron is a sturdy option for lamps and wall lighting. As with all aspects of rustic décor, the lighting should have some connection to nature, with both lamp base and shade being of natural materials.

★ When picking accessories for your rustic space, feel free to take the project in whatever direction you feel represents your idea of the rustic lifestyle. If a ranch or fishing-camp motif doesn't suit you, possibly a mountain or Adirondack-retreat style is a match for your taste. Whatever theme you choose, have fun collecting objects that reveal your fantasies, that tell where you'd rather be if you had your wishes.

resources

HERE IS A SAMPLING OF PLACES THAT OFFER
WESTERN OR RUSTIC-STYLE FURNISHINGS
AND ACCESSORIES.

ABC Carpet

881 & 888 Broadway at E 19th St
New York, NY 10003
www.abchome.com

*All nature of furnishings, accessories,
and floor coverings.*

The Annex Flea Market

26th and 6th St
New York, NY 10116
212-243-5343

*A wide variety of vendors, many with
western or rustic one-of-a-kinds.*

Antèks Home Furnishings

(7 locations)

8466 Melrose Ave
Los Angeles, CA 90069
323-653-0810

*Western and rustic furnishings and
accessories, one-of-a-kind collectibles,
lighting, rugs, tableware, and bedding.*

3112 Piedmont Rd NE
Atlanta, GA 30305
404-233-6675

4646 J. C. Nichols Pkwy
Kansas City, MO 64112
816-561-7757

5814 W Lovers Ln
Dallas, TX 75225
214.528.5567

2545 Kirby Dr
Houston, TX 77098
713-526-4800

2208 Dallas Pkwy
Plano, TX 75293
972-378-0853

6547 San Pedro
San Antonio, TX 78216
210-348-6460

Back at the Ranch

209 Marcy
Santa Fe, NM 87501
505-989-8180

*Vintage boots and cowboy hats,
blankets and bandanas.*

Big Creek Willow

S 15495 Canary Dr
Strum, WI 54770
715-695-3318

Bent willow and birch-bark furniture.

Brimfield Antiques Show

Brimfield, MA
413-283-2418

*Several shows make up this huge market,
held twice yearly. Great source for rustic
and cabin décor.*

Covert Workshops

2007 Public St

Cody, WY 82414

307-527-5964

Handcrafted Molesworth and cowboy-style furniture of burl wood, featuring leather trim and beadwork.

Indian Territory

1212 Sheridan Ave

Cody, WY 82414

307-527-5584

www.indianterritorycody.com

Native American arts and artifacts, wholesale and retail.

Into the West

907 Lincoln Ave

Steamboat Springs, CO 80488

970-879-8377

Cowboy-style furnishings and accessories.

Jackson Moore, Ltd.

130 E Broadway

PO Box 12229

Jackson, WY 83002

800-667-4616

www.jacksonmoore.com

Complete turnkey projects a specialty. Both upholstery and case goods.

Laguna Vintage Pottery

116 S Washington St

Seattle, WA 98104

206-682-6162

Vintage dinnerware, pottery, and linens.

Minnewaska Rustics

20903 S Lakeshore Dr

Glenwood, MN 56334

320-634-3947

Twig, tramp art, and cowboy furnishings and accessories.

New West

2811 Big Horn Ave

Cody, WY 82414

800-653-2391

www.newest.com

Furniture in the tradition of Thomas Molesworth.

Ralph Kylloe Gallery

PO Box 669

Lake George, NY 12845

518-696-4100

www.ralphkylloe.com

Adirondack and western décor, antique boats, antler lighting, and accessories.

The Ranch Home Furnishings

1331 Texas Ave

El Paso, TX 79901

915-544-0865

email: theranch@dzn.com

Western and rustic furnishings and accessories to the trade only.

Red Nations Art

PO Box 388

Lander, WY 82520

307-332-2134

*Museum-quality cultural art in the style
of the High Plains people.*

Replacements Ltd.

PO Box 26029

Greensboro, NC 27420

336-697-3000

www.replacements.com

*Vintage china and tableware to complete
a set or start new.*

Rocketbuster Boot Company

115 S Anthony

El Paso, TX 79901

915-541-1300

www.rocketbuster.com

*Tooled and inlaid leather pillows and table
runners, plus fine boots, many in
vintage styles.*

Rosebowl Flea Market

1001 Rosebowl Dr

Pasadena, CA 90031

213-560-7469

www.rgcshows.com/rosebowl.asp

*Possibly the world's hippest flea market!
Who knows what you may find?*

Ruby Montana's Pinto Pony

Coral Sands Inn

210 W Stevens Rd

Palm Springs, CA 92262

760-325-4900

www.rubymontana.com

*Western and cowboy kitsch, collectibles
and décor.*

SweetTree Rustic

PO Box 1827

Tonasket, WA 98855

509-486-1573

Twig furniture with a tramp-art flair.

Viers Montana Western Company

65 Billman Ln

Livingston, MT 59047

406-222-7564

email: info@montanawesternfurn.com

*Handcrafted western furniture in the
Molesworth style.*

World Famous First Monday Trade Days

Canton, TX

903-567-6015

www.firstmonday.com

*The ultimate flea market! More than
8,500 spaces rented in peak months.
Whatever you are looking for is here.
It will take two or three days to hike
the market, however.*

**Yocham's Custom Leather
and Saddlery & Cowboy Décor**

Rt 1 Box 536-A

Bartlesville, OK 74006

918-335-2277

email: yochams@fullnet.net

*Tooled leather, cowhide, and horn
furniture. All manner of cowboy gear.*